Deeply Rooted

Deeply Rooted

Copyright © 2025 Jametria Mays
All rights reserved.

No part of this book may be reproduced, distributed, or transmitted in any form or by any means—electronic, mechanical, photocopying, recording, or otherwise—without prior written permission of the author, except for brief quotations used in reviews or scholarly works.

This book is a work of nonfiction. The events and experiences described are true to the best of the author's memory. Names, locations, and identifying details may have been changed to protect the privacy of individuals.

The prayers, poems, and reflections included are personal expressions of the author's lived experience and are not intended to replace professional, medical, legal, or therapeutic advice.

Printed in the United States of America

ISBN 979-8-90243-861-8

ISBN: 9798245389103

Deeply Rooted
A Journal-Style Memoir of Stories and Poems

Jametria Mays

Deeply Rooted

Deeply Rooted

Be your true, authentic self.

This isn't just any book. This is my journal.

There's no such thing as a perfect story. Life doesn't happen in order, and healing definitely doesn't.

These are short stories from different moments of my life I wrote while I was trying to heal—sometimes without knowing how. Writing was how I survived what I was going through at the moment.

Some are heavy. Some are prayers or poems I wrote when I didn't know what else to say. None of this is meant to be polished, just real..

I share experiences with neglect, abuse, motherhood, marriage, and the sacrifices that come with trying to keep going when life feels heavy. This book isn't about having it all figured out. It's about showing up anyway.

The name *Deeply Rooted* comes from the truth that so much of my adult life was shaped by my childhood. The way I loved, the way i think, the way I protected myself. and what I've allowed.

At times I gave too much. Other times I became heartless.

Welcome to Meme's world.

Deeply Rooted

Deeply Rooted

Table of Contents

Chapter One — *Break or Be Broken* 1

Chapter Two — *50 Shades of Roses* 11

Poem Break — *I'm a Survivor* 26

Chapter Three — *Depression.* 31

Chapter Four — *KYSS.* 41

Chapter Five — *Fake Ass Marriage* 49

Chapter Six — *Contemplation* 57

Chapter Seven — *Scared and Lonely* 69

Poem Break — *Scared and Lonely* 78

Chapter Eight — *Stability.* 79

Chapter Nine — *Jealousy in Disguise* 85

Chapter Ten — *I Thought He Loved Me* 97

Prayer Break — *Praying for Peace* 105

Deeply Rooted

Deeply Rooted

Chapter Eleven — *Over It (Crash Out Session)* 109

Poem Break — *Funny Business* 115

Chapter Twelve — *Imperfections* 121

Chapter Thirteen — *Re.Soul* 127

Poem Break — *Re Soul* 135

Chapter Fourteen — *Meme's Prayer* 141

Chapter Fifteen — *Me vs Them* 147

Chapter Sixteen — *Self Love Over Survival* 161

Chapter Seventeen — *Diamond Necklace* 165

Poem Braek- *WTF* 179

Chapter Eighteen — *Bad Days...* 183

Chapter Nineteen — *Deeply — A Life Deeply Rooted.* 191

Closing Treatment — *Diary* 203

Deeply Rooted

Deeply Rooted

Father God,

Please protect me and my family. I come to You with open arms, and I give You my past. Please continue to guide me down the path You've chosen for me, and help me understand my purpose.

I need You every day — especially on the days I forget to pray.

Sometimes I feel like so many people are against me, trying to destroy me. Maybe it's just my mind playing tricks on me because of all the anxiety I've carried through my life. But that's okay, because I know you've got me no matter what.

Still, I need You. I need Your protection, Your love, and Your guidance.

I've let go of my past to make room for a new life, but I'm still lost. I still don't have it all figured out. I still make unnecessary mistakes.

Every day I face obstacles, and I often ask myself if I'll make it through this one.

With You, I know anything is possible, but I'm still human. Sometimes I still have doubts and fears.

Please give me the strength to keep going. Help me to trust You more, even when I can't see the way.

In Jesus' name, I pray. Amen.

Dedicated to Children
Jordan, Chanel and Kailah

Love Always

Chapter one
Break or be broken

Deeply Rooted

Growing up, I endured so much betrayal, pain, anger, confusion, and frustration. I never really understood my emotions, let alone knew how to control them. I was raised in Richmond, CA. We didn't have much, but my family always stuck together and looked out for one another. If my mother couldn't provide, we had my grandmother, her boyfriend at the time who I looked up to as a grandfather., or my aunts. We lived all over Richmond, borderline poor, but the days I remember most are my Crescent Park days.

My parents used to party a lot when we lived in the Crescent. I was about nine years old, and I remember there always being people over. We were told to stay in our rooms, but of course we didn't listen. Because of that, we witnessed our parents' doing drugs and drinking. Tweaking out. At the time, I didn't think anything of it. It never really bothered us because it gave us room to do whatever we wanted.

A lot of shit went down. But there's one night I'll never forget. The night my dad made his way into my bedroom. At first, I thought he was just drunk and forgot where his room was. He would lay there, drunk and high as fuck, then leave after a few hours. But after the third time, he started touching me. I was confused, but I knew it wasn't right. I was just too afraid to say anything.

My mother was in a very abusive relationship. I watched him beat on her several times—behind closed doors and in front of other people. He was a fucking monster. I didn't want to say anything to my mother and risk her getting beat if she confronted him. I'll never forget walking into the bathroom and seeing my mother throwing up blood, or the time he beat her outside while the neighbors watched. I was always so scared for my mom, and that shit fucked with me, so I stayed quiet.

Years went by, and he continued to rape me. I remained silent. I was scared and embarrassed, especially after it happened so many times.

I remember one time my cousin was over for the night, and he tried touching her. She immediately rejected him and told her parents. The topic came up, but I don't remember what came of it because nothing ever happened. Our parents continued partying together. I honestly believe I was too far gone at that point. Both of our parents were battling drug and alcohol abuse, so who really knows. But one thing I know for sure—my cousin never forgot.

Deeply Rooted

We didn't talk about it again until I finally spoke up. She called me and told me how proud she was that I finally told the truth. But if I'm being honest, I still don't think my family believed me or even cared. To this day, she reminds me how strong I am and encourages me to keep going. I appreciate her because she kept all my secrets. We were close in age but raised differently. She had her beliefs, and I had mine, yet she never judged me for the fucked-up shit she witnessed me do. I can truly say she was my first best friend.

We moved around a lot, so I had many friends and associates from all over, but I don't think they really knew me. We were young, just outside living our little lives. My Crescent Park besties were a whole vibe, though, and we still have love for each other to this day, even if we only talk from time to time.

Then I met Laura. We met at a new school in Sacramento and instantly connected. We were both from Richmond and had Hella shit in common. One time, I got caught with some boys in my mom's house while she was at work. My brother called my cousins, and they told my aunt. Laura, the two boys, and I were hanging out in my room when my aunt and cousins burst in, tripping the fuck out. She didn't play—she beat my ass right in front of everyone. Embarrassing as hell, honestly.

After that, my mom came home and called my dad to come "handle" me. He drove all the way from Richmond just to beat my ass again. He was throwing irons and all kinds of shit at me while my mom sat in the other room and let it happen. Eventually she came in and told him to stop. But I was still crushed, mostly because all I could think was that the only reason he was mad was because he wanted to be the only one touching me. There were times he even asked me to perform oral sex on him because he didn't want me to get pregnant, but i refused... What a fucking pedophile.

That day, I realized I no longer wanted to live with my mom or be around either of them. It wasn't because I got caught with boys—I was only fourteen and had no business laying up with anyone—but after being raped for so long, I felt grown. I felt like I could do whatever I wanted.

For a short moment, he was gone, and I felt free—until my mom called him back and I had to pretend to be ok. I never felt protected by her. Most of my childhood, I felt like she disliked me and knew exactly what was happening to me.

I wanted to be normal so bad. When I finally had sex by choice, outside of my dad raping me, I told the guy I was a virgin and that he was my first. In a way, he was—because it was my choice. Technically, I didn't lie. Still, it was a sick feeling.

I didn't really blame my mother until I got older and had children of my own. Now I can't help but wonder how she didn't protect me. Especially because I was convinced that she knew what was going on. I mean how could she not? I remember one night she found him sleep in my bed and she did nothing, Just woke him up and proceeded to direct him into their bedroom… I pay attention to everything when it comes to my daughters—their body language, attitudes, especially when men are around. I would literally go to war behind mine. I'm constantly checking in with them, asking if they're comfortable, making sure they know they can tell me anything—especially if a grown man even looks at them funny.

I believe they would tell me if something happened, but I still fear they might not. What I do know is I never want them to feel how I felt.

Deeply Rooted

I was sexually abused for years, and no one knew. It took me going to jail when I was 18 and a therapist asking about my upbringing for everything to come out. I don't know what came over me, but I told her everything. I felt so relieved. From that point on, I moved differently and completely cut my dad out of my life.

I still didn't tell my mom then. I didn't want to hurt her, and so much time had passed that I didn't think she would believe me anyway. She was still dealing with him on and off, so I assumed she wouldn't care. My sisters eventually found out, but they still praised him— "my dad this, my dad that." It always irritated me hearing them brag about their relationship with him.

Then one day, my mom randomly called and asked me about it. I told her everything. I assumed she heard it from one of my sisters. I cried for weeks after that conversation. Once again, I felt like the talk of the family. Once again, I felt like "the problem."

I still don't feel compassion or concern from my mother—not because I'm looking for sympathy, but because I expected more. Maybe understanding. Maybe a better relationship.

Deeply Rooted

Once I stopped being ashamed and started telling my story, I realized I wasn't alone. So many women have experienced sexual abuse in the home or by someone they trusted. That shit is sad as fuck. It happens so often it almost feels normal—but it shouldn't be.

I always wanted to write about it or get into film and turn my experiences into a script. Sometimes I thought, who even cares? Maybe that thought came from the people who should have cared never showing up. But fuck that—this is my story, and this is part of my healing.

Writing helped me realize I wasn't alone and had nothing to be ashamed of. We all have stories, and so many of them are painfully similar. I've read books and watched movies about this same topic and still wonder what the fuck is really going on. There isn't enough awareness or protection for young people experiencing sexual abuse.

I tried therapy, but it never really worked for me. As a teen, I had been through so much that I grew numb. Pain, betrayal, disrespect—nothing really fazed me anymore. I lived with a fake smile and a prayer.

Deeply Rooted

Writing became my therapy. Not quite journaling, but close. Like many of us, I leaned into liquor and men for comfort and security, but it was always temporary. Honestly, I don't know if I'll ever fully heal from all the trauma. But I've accomplished a lot, and I never let my past define my future.

When shit gets tough, I don't fold. I cry, but I keep pushing. I've been figuring life out on my own since I was a teen. When I left home, I promised myself I'd never return. That place breaks me and forces me to face all my past trauma. It constantly reminds me how undervalued I felt.

Now I have children of my own. My girls are teens, and they need me more than ever. The place I once called home still breaks me the most, but I refuse to be broken. I choose to break through every obstacle life puts in front of me.

And to every woman who has experienced sexual abuse and a lack of protection: **WE ARE NOT VICTIMS. WE ARE VICTORS.** You are not alone. And you got this.

Deeply Rooted

Chapter two

50 Shades of Roses

Deeply Rooted

I wanted to support a cause and bring more awareness to women who share experiences similar to mine, so I decided to start a nonprofit organization called **50 Shades of Roses**, designed to help abused and battered women. I chose the name because roses are my favorite flowers, and each color represents a different meaning. Each one expressing emotions As I researched them, I discovered there were 50 shade I've personally experienced.

Aside from the sexual abuse I endured as a minor, I got married very young at the age of 19 to Albert. At the time, I didn't know any better. I truly believed this guy loved me. I was only 16 when we first met in high school, and he had been trying to get with me ever since. I was friends with his sister, and he would always flirt, but nothing ever happened because I was on some other shit. I was deeply in love with this older guy named Sean. Sean was all over the place also—baby mama drama, street shit, all of that. He was from Richmond, fine as fuck, and I had no business liking him, but I did.

Years later, Albert and I ran into each other at the mall. He was home on college break, and I was out here running the streets, not really doing much with myself if I'm being honest. We ended up realizing it was both of our birthdays that day, so we instantly connected. We hung out a few times—nothing major, just some car sex and late-night conversations. A few months later, I found out I was pregnant.

I was terrified to tell anyone. My aunt caught on and personally took me to get a pregnancy test, so I couldn't hide it anymore. Around that same time, I was still messing with Sean and didn't want to lose him. Even though I was pretty sure he wasn't the father, So i let Sean believe there was a possibility the baby was his. Sean knew it was a 50/50 chance, but Albert didn't, so the pregnancy was weird as hell. I literally had two baby daddies for 9 months. Shit was wild

After I gave birth to my baby boy, Albert proposed. His family wasn't supportive at all. In fact, his mom hated it. It was clear that she didn't like me and felt I wasn't a good fit for him. She only tolerated me because of the baby. However, there were times I had nowhere to live because me and my mom was never able to get alone. I'm almost convince she hated me too but anyway I stayed with albert at his mom's house; she had some Strick rules and wouldn't allow us to sleep together in the same room because we weren't married. So one day we randomly decided to go to the courthouse and get married. Looking back, I think we did it to prove a point—not out of genuine love. We were young, confused, and just trying to do what we thought was right.

For a moment, I felt happy. I envisioned a fairytale ending—a stable home, both parents present, a healthy environment for my child the whole shit. But That vision didn't last long.

When my baby was a few months old, I took him to Detroit to meet Albert's dad's side of the family. I was terrified flying alone with a baby for the first time. When I arrived, his dad picked us up in this pimped-out van with a big-ass TV mounted inside, at the time that was some shit I've never seen before so I instantly felt this would be a cool experience. His dad greeted us with so much love and took us to get food from this Detroit's famous coney island spot. Yes, the food was good as hell, they had the best chili cheese fries I have ever tasted besides Nations in Richmond lol.. His Detroit family welcomed me with open arms, and for the first time in a long time, I felt genuine family love.

A few days later, Albert started showing his ass and his true colors came out. We were at his dad's condo with his siblings, joking and talking shit. Although we were friends in the past, I was almost convinced they really didn't really like me neither, and he started disrespecting me in front of them so i talked my shit back, and he didn't like that. He pushed me down aggressively. That was the first time a man ever physically assaulted me besides my dad. I was in shock.

It was snowing outside, freezing cold, but I left the condo alone. I walked for blocks before realizing I had nowhere to go. I sat inside of a coney island fast-food restaurant for hours, hurt and angry, wishing he would come after me. He never did. When I eventually went back, we both acted like nothing happened.

Things only got worse. He continued physically abusing me. A year later, I got into some legal trouble and needed to lay low, so we went back to Detroit. His dad's side of the family knew my flaws and never judged me, so the transition went smoothly. They tried to help me get my shit together and taught me more survival skills in a different surrounding. Although I was born and raised in the Bay Area and had my share of survival techniques, But Detroit was something different. I became more exposed to a different lifestyle. I landed a job at Footaction in Eastland Mall and started feeling at home. I fell in love with Detroit and was open to staying for a while.

My Baby daddy hated that shit. When we first arrived in Detroit, we stayed at his grandmother's house but after a few months we moved in with his aunt, and that's when shit got messy. He hated all the love I was being shown because he was too busy trying to put me down all the time. I must admit that I may be partial to blame because I allowed myself to participate in shit, I knew he would like. shit I can't help that everyone liked me. I believe his aunt hated that shit too. This chic was always on some fake shit, pretending to be a solid woman whole time she was a manipulative sneaky bitch. She would claim to care for me but would take me to her old job at a strip club trying to convince me that I should dance, introduce me to men with money all just to run back to her nephew and gossip like i was out here being in other niggas faces while he was at home with our baby. "Being a good husband" I never liked living with her but my Baby daddy loved it. My goal was to make enough money to move so that I wouldn't have to deal with her fake ass anymore. One day after working long hours. I came home from work to find out he had moved back to California—and took my baby with him. I was livid. His aunt played both sides, pretending to support me while telling him I was no good and convinces him to leave me without any warning. Knowing I had nowhere to go. I was so scared to stay but was more afraid to go back to Cali, so His dad and stepmom offered for me to live with them until I found a place, I guess they felt bad for me. I accepted the offer because they had always treated me with respect, but being away from my son broke me. I spiraled and became a different person. I must admit that shit changed me, I became even more heartless than before.

Eventually, I went back to California, cleared my name, and was put on an ankle monitor for a few months. During that time back fucking with my baby daddy I got pregnant again. This time It was a high-risk pregnancy. I was constantly sick, in and out of the hospital, on bed rest— But that didn't stop him from still beating on me. I went into early labor, and my daughter ended up in the NICU for a month. One day while I was pumping milk, he told me if our daughter died, he would kill me. Like first of all why would he event think some shit like that.

As he continues with the madness shit just kept getting worst. It's like the longer I stayed with him the more aggressive he became. After time progressed I became fed up, I was over the abuse, so I moved with my mom and started hanging out with old friends, but he was not having that shit neither. I had an OG Patna that use to let me drive his Benz or his Mustang around because I didn't have my own car at the time. Crazy part is that he didn't even want shit from me but to ride out to the bay area with him from time to time while he made his runs. He was cool tho and I was really feeling myself at that time. Meanwhile baby daddy would always be at his mom's house with the kids. He never had shit going on for real. One day he got so upset that he asked me to pull up on him so I did, we drove to get something to eat then he asked me to pull over so we could talk. While we were just sitting in silence he Pulls out his gun and points it at me then tells me to show him where my OG friend lives, he was scaring the shit out of me, so I did what he asked. I didn't want to expose my friend whereabouts, so I took him to some random house on the opposite side of town. He knocked on the door and thankfully no one was home because only God knows how that could have ended. On the way back I remember him talking shit and constantly hitting me in my face anytime I responded so I stopped, jumped out of the car then called my grandmother to pick me up. When she arrived, she didn't ask any questions and just took me home. When we arrived at the house, I started to explain what happened and she stopped me mid conversation and asked me if I was going to leave him. I didn't respond fast enough I guess so she proceeded to say that he's my husband and I am to just do as he say and to let it go, the same response I got from her when I found out he was fucking my cousin... At that moment I was reminded that I'm still alone out here no matter what. Nobody cares. Later that day I called my friend, and he went to go pick up the car and brought it back to me. He was a real one and he never judge me just gave me some decent advice and kept it moving. I mean of course he liked me, but he was old, and I just really wanted the money and to have a car to drive so I'll just act interested but not enough to have sex with him. he knew that though, but he never questioned anything or felt any kind of way. After that moment time past and I had stopped talking to him. Partially because I didn't want him getting involved with my drama, but we always remained good friends. I began working for this insurance company and went back to school. Things seemed to feel normal until I ended up pregnant again this time it was an ectopic pregnancy, and

Deeply Rooted

I had miscarried. Baby daddy blamed me for that shit also…

One day I remember sitting in the room watching TV, and this man came in mad for absolutely no reason. I didn't budge or argue, but to be honest, I was scared. Me not reacting made him even more mad. He jumped on the bed, slammed me into the pillows, then threw me on the floor and started punching me. I screamed that I was pregnant and wasn't feeling well. I lied in that moment just to stop him from attacking me—but to my surprise, I really was pregnant.

After telling him I was pregnant, I scheduled a doctor visit just to keep my story going. The plan was to tell him I miscarried again, but I was actually pregnant. Six months into my pregnancy, my brother got into some trouble and needed somewhere to hide out. I didn't want him in Sacramento to get caught, so my baby daddy and I arranged for him to go to Atlanta, where his sisters already lived.

We were planning to move there after I had the baby and saved more money, but a week later we said fuck it, packed my entire apartment, and moved to Atlanta pregnant and all. Our first few weeks in Atlanta were really cool—

peaceful—and he wasn't hitting me. He was still verbally abusive, but compared to before, it felt like nothing. I was called every name in the book, but I had become numb to it. Verbal abuse had become normal to me.

When we got to Atlanta, he didn't have shit going on, per usual. I was pregnant and hustling daily to provide for our family. He was trying to focus on a rap career and sell weed here and there, but I was out bringing in the money—scamming and more. Most of the abuse in Atlanta came from jealousy. Everything we had; I got. He was basically the house mom, but he didn't care.

I remember one day going out for a girls' night. At first, he seemed cool with it since I was with his sisters. My phone died, so we stopped at a pay phone to call him so that he wouldn't think anything weird. Over the phone, he acted fine. When I got home, he was outside smoking and asked if I had fun. I told him we had a ball.

The moment I walked inside, he slammed the door and attacked me in front of my daughters. My son stayed in the room and wouldn't come out. I remember laying on the floor while he kicked me in the head and stomach, begging God to save me. That was the first time I felt like I was going to die—and to this day, I feel like a part of me did.

After that, I tried everything not to trigger him. I was scared to do anything. On my youngest daughter's first birthday, we planned a small gathering. Again, he was annoyed for no reason. Some of my family members had mentioned that he was using drugs, but I never believed it but now the more I think about it maybe he was and that was the reason he would tweak out. I went upstairs to avoid embarrassment, but here he goes following me with the bullshit. We argued, he got loud so everyone could hear, then beat my ass again. That time I screamed for help in hopes that someone would come stop him, but no one came. His sisters and friends heard everything and did nothing. He even tried to bite my fingers off. The attempt alone was insane.

Later, he met some people with money and "business opportunities." They were scammers, moving around a lot, and he followed them. As long as he was bringing money home, I didn't care. Eventually he moved to Vegas with them and left me and the kids in Atlanta. I moved his sister and her baby daddy in because at the time they were homeless, although albert was supposed to be making money he still didn't provide so I was also hoping for his sister to pitch in on some bills or something. but she never paid anything. I got evicted and now We were all homeless. I stayed in hotels for about two weeks before he invited us to Vegas.

In the beginning Vegas was weird. We lived in a big house with 6 other people. We were told to stay in the room while they worked. He acted like he was part of some mafia and said leaving would put us in danger. he would say stupid shit like that he didn't really trust these guys but if he was to leave, we could be in harms way. So, I just went with it even though it didn't make any sense to me. One day I remember him going off and me being in the same situation that I was in when we lived in Atlanta with screaming for help, this time he broke my nose. So, I ran outside for help and after running a few blocks I was able call the paramedics, they came and took me to the hospital because my nose wouldn't stop bleeding. the police came to get a statement but of course I lied. When I was released from the hospital, I called this girl I had recently met and asked her to come pick me up, I never went back to that house. I was staying with her for a few days so that my son could stay in school. one day I went to pick him up and this nigga was there waiting on me. He didn't cause a big scene but that alone was enough for me to move around... his friend guided my son into the car that they were in and I just got into my friends car and we just left, The next day I had the police escort me to get my son and some things out of that house then my friend took me straight to the airport. I went back to Cali for about 2 weeks to gather my thoughts while I found a place for me and my kids to live. I came back to Vegas and moved into my own shit this time. I chose to come back to Las Vegas because I wanted to pursue my business as a swimsuit designer, and I didn't want to live back in Cali...

It's crazy how sometimes we just don't get it, we don't value ourselves enough to understand what's happening. the desperation for love is real, being delusional is a real thing, lust and obsession is a real thing. All the red flags could be staring us right in the face but yet we will still not see them, or we chose to ignore them in hopes of a different outcome, hoping that maybe, just maybe this time around would be different. We will do anything just to say we have someone with the knowledge of knowing that they are not good for us. I created 50 shades of roses to help women that have been and still is in the same situations I was in. We need more support and guidance even if we refuse to say so. We need to feel protected and loved by the one who claim to love us. We often turn back to our abusers because they manipulate us in to believing the impossible of change behavior. This man could have killed me on so may occasions and I still stuck around due to lack of self love and self-respect. It's easier said that done but it's the truth. I don't wish that pain on anyone and I wish that more women to stand for one another. I have witnessed to many women laughing at another's pain and trauma and its really mind bothering.

I pray that one day we are more understood instead of being looked at as problems because we lack the knowledge of knowing how to handle our emotions. Thou shall not judge. Right? It ok to be kind because you never know what someone's else is going through. For a long time, I was ashamed to tell my story. I didn't want to be looked at as a victim or broken because I don't view myself that way. I'm a survivor, and I will always stand on that.

I'm no longer ashamed, nor do I punish myself for staying. It's over, and I made it through, and that's all that matters.

I'm a Survivor

To the ones who learned silence
before they learned safety,
who mastered survival
in rooms where love came with bruises.

To the ones who stayed—not because they were weak,
but because hope can sound like promises
when fear is loud
and escape feels impossible or to deep.

To the ones called dramatic, difficult, broken,
when really you were bleeding in pieces,
quietly coping,
still showing up, still holding it together
while the world kept asking
why you weren't better.

Listen—

Deeply Rooted

You are not the chaos they caused.
You are not the hands that hurt you.
You are not the names screamed at you
in moments meant to erase you.

You are breath after impact.
You are courage disguised as endurance.
You are proof that the body remembers how to live
even when the heart is tired.

Some of you left.
Some of you are still planning.
Some of you survived in pieces
and are learning how to gather yourselves
again.

There is no shame in staying.
There is no timeline on healing.
There is no single way to be free.

Let the world know this:
You are not a victim—you are a witness.

Deeply Rooted

A witness to pain,
and to the miracle of still being here.

And when your voice shakes,
when your story comes out in fragments,
know that every word is sacred
and every step forward counts.

You are seen.
You are believed.
You are loved—without conditions, without fear.

And one day, when you look back,
you will not only see what you survived—
you will see who you became.

A survivor.
A warrior.
A light that refused to go out.

50 Shades of Roses *is a non-profit organization for abused and battered women. My goal is to form a support group to help women get out of situations that are harming them mentally, physically, and emotionally. I pray that my story can help others understand that they are not alone and that they, too, can get away from their abuser. We are survivors, and we* **WILL WIN**!

Love yourself enough to let go…

Deeply Rooted

Chapter three
Depression

Deeply Rooted

I hate it here...
Not just *here* as in a place, but here in this era, this time, this version of the world where nothing feels genuine anymore. Everything feels transactional. Everyone is out for themselves, and nobody really gives a fuck about anyone unless there's something to gain. Relationships feel circumstantial. Conditional. Temporary. And honestly, that shit is sad to me.

The longer time goes on, the worse it gets. We're living in a world with no values. Marriage doesn't mean commitment anymore. Having kids has turned into a strategy instead of a responsibility—sometimes just a way to trap someone for financial security if you "bag the right one." Blood relatives grow distant. Real friendships barely exist. Loyalty feels rare. Integrity feels extinct. And somehow, if you don't adapt, you get drowned out. If you don't speak up for yourself or jump out of character, you're invisible.

This world is cold, and if you let it, it will break you.

I've suffered in every way possible—mentally, physically, emotionally, financially. And some days I genuinely don't know how I'm still standing.

Deeply Rooted

When I was a teenager, my best friend and I used to hang around older guys. We didn't care about age back then— shit we thought we were grown. One night at a party, one of the guys laced a bottle of gin or orange juice. I still don't know how they did it. We never left our drinks unattended. One minute we were drinking and smoking, the next minute everything went left. I remember tripping the fuck out. Most of that night is blank.

The next day I was still high. I went to my mom's house to shower and change, and a few hours later I collapsed on her stairs. My brother found me and was rushed to the hospital. When I woke up, the doctor told me my blood work came back positive for meth. I was confused. Scared and Ashamed. When I talked to my friend, I learned she experienced the same thing. Another one of our home girls that was at the same party later told us she had been drugged and raped that night also.

We never reported it. Not because it wasn't serious, but because we were kids who didn't have people who cared enough to protect us or guide us through it. We kept a lot from our parents —but they knew enough to be concerned. And they weren't.

My friend's mom tried to help us through some of those moments, but for the most part, she pretty much allowed us to do whatever we wanted. I stayed with them from time to time because she would basically let us live alone in their apartment. We had niggas staying with us and everything. She was the cool mom and I truly believe that she wanted us to be safe at all times, but we were too wild to listen...

I remember one night we were out, and one of the guys convinced us to try an ecstasy pill. We did. At first, we didn't feel anything, so we kept partying like nothing happened. But when we went back to the apartment, it finally hit us—and we tripped the fuck out. This time, her mom was there. She gave us some milk and walked us around the block a few times, trying to calm us down.

I remember feeling like a crackhead. And I guess we looked the part, because while we were walking, some niggas rolled up on us. At first, they were trying to holla, but then they straight-up asked if we had swallowed some crack rocks. We burst out laughing—completely unserious—even though, deep down, we felt like we were going to die.

Deeply Rooted

I've had other drug-related experiences that terrified me enough to stay away from strong drugs entirely.

here's a day I remember clear as hell—my father and my aunt were hanging out at my granny's house in Richmond. They were drinking, doing drugs and shit, acting like everything was normal. At some point, my dad handed me a little baggie with some weed and told me to go smoke…

I rolled up and went into my granny's garage to smoke. Almost immediately, I started freaking out. My heart was racing, my chest felt tight, and I didn't know what the fuck was happening to me. I went to the bathroom to wash my face, hoping it would help. But when I looked at myself in the mirror, I swear I saw a demon staring back at me. That shit scared the fuck out of me. I don't know if what they gave me was laced or what, but I was gone an didn't like the shit.

I don't even know how long I was in that bathroom. When I finally came out, I still tweaking but was trying to act normal, my aunt handed me a drink—Seagram's gin mixed with Remy Red and told me to drink it to calm down. And I did. I trusted her…

Not long after that, my dad asked me if I wanted to learn how to drive a stick shift. I got excited. Thinking it was something normal. Something a dad would do with his kid. But it wasn't that at all. That was just another way he lured me into the car—another setup that ended in him raping me.

Being slipped shit without consent, Betrayed, hallucinating, seeing demons in the mirror—it changes you. It creates fear. Distrust. Hyper-vigilance. To this day, I'm more scared of my kids experiencing that shit than anything else, which is why I'm painfully honest with them. Some people say I'm too open, but I don't give a fuck. I wish someone had been open with me.

That's how trauma starts. Quietly. Unaddressed. And it doesn't disappear—it embeds itself into your nervous system.

And trauma doesn't just stay in the past. It shows up later as anxiety, panic attacks, insomnia, depression, hyper-independence, self-sabotage, emotional numbness, and constant survival mode. Depression isn't just sadness. It's exhaustion. It's waking up already tired. It's forcing yourself out of bed because other people depend on you. It's functioning while falling apart. It's smiling in public and crying alone in the shower.

I've been sexually assaulted many more times as an adult— one time by my boss. When I tried to report it, they flipped the script. Denied everything then Retaliated and Accused me of stealing benefits. It was their way of winning the retaliation lawsuit, but it was all Lies. I had proof But because of my past, I didn't have a leg to stand on. When I attempted to speak up about it in court The judge saw my history and stopped listening. My case was voided and my abuser walked free.

That's when you really start questioning whether we even have rights.

They say we do but do we really?

Depression deepened after that and I felt triggered all over again, I drink almost a bottle of wine a day just to cope. Sometimes it's the only way I can sleep. My anxiety stays on ten. Panic attacks come out of nowhere. My doctor tried prescribing me with meds to help but after all the bad experiences with drugs I was too afraid to take them. I don't like feeling high but sometimes a low dose of indica would help slow my thoughts enough to breathe. I hate that I need anything at all just to feel okay.

But I'm tired… I'm going through another divorce. Past trauma keeps resurfacing. I've now been displaced from my home. I'm dealing with lawsuits, legal issues, failed investments, business stress, financial strain, and parenting teenagers who are struggling themselves emotionally and it hurts that some days I don't know how to help them. Depression makes everything heavier. It clouds judgment. It steals motivation. It makes simple tasks feel impossible.

Some days I cry just trying to shower.

I've isolated myself. No friends. Limited family. The one person I thought would stay turned their back on me. I deactivated my social media, and even though I'm still trying to run a business. That decision saved my peace but hurt my visibility. Depression makes you want to disappear—even when you know you shouldn't.

Depression also lies. It tells you you're failing. That you're not enough. That nothing will work out. That God isn't listening and That the pain won't end.

Deeply Rooted

And when you've lived a life full of betrayal, abuse, and disappointment, it's hard not to question your existence. You tend to feel punished instead of protected.

But here's the truth that depression doesn't want you to remember:

You are still here.
You are still trying.
You are still showing up for your kids.
You are still building, even while breaking.

Depression is real. It's a disease. And if left unchecked, it will take over your life. But it can be managed. Through honesty. Through boundaries. Through therapy. Through community. Through rest. Through self-compassion. Through refusing to give up— even when you want to.

If you're dealing with depression, please know this: you are not weak. You are not broken. You are not alone. Your struggle is valid. Your pain matters and Healing is not chronological.

Every struggle becomes a testimony if you survive it and if nobody's told you today— I'm proud of you.

Keep going You're stronger than you think.

Deeply Rooted

Chapter Four
KYSS (Keep Yourself sexy)
Building the Brand

I'll never forget the day I decided to start my brand. I'd wanted to own a boutique most of my life, but designing? That was something I never thought I'd actually do—until one day in Atlanta. I went to a fashion show—so much fun—and experiencing it from backstage, interacting with the designers, feeling the energy, I just knew. Right then and there, I decided that's what I wanted to do.

The show was all about women's dresses and dope fashion, but I wanted something different, something I didn't see much of—swimwear. When I moved to Las Vegas and realized the city was filled with pool parties and endless opportunities to sell swimwear, I was ready. I remember sitting in my room, mapping out my entire plan. I got online, designed my logo, created business cards, bought fabric, booked some ladies off Craigslist to model my brand— and went crazy. In the beginning, nobody could tell me shit, especially once I started actually making money off my designs.

I eventually built a team of women who modeled for music videos, reality shows, and even a few movies. We did all kinds of showcases and fashion shows—I had my team booked and busy. Most of the time, we got paid, but often it was for trades. At that time, we didn't know any better; we were all learning the business, figuring out how it worked, and slowly realizing that the people we were doing free work for were just playing us. A few of my ladies fell off, but I kept some solid ones around.

There was this one model who danced at a local gentlemen's club. She started selling my pieces to some of the other ladies at the club. I'll forever fuck with her for that because she wasn't making much money, but she was committed to pushing my brand. I'll never forget that loyalty.

About a year into running my brand, I went through a breakup from a long-term relationship—my marriage—and I felt a little discouraged. For the first time in a long while, I felt alone. I still had my ladies around, but no family, no real friends. I didn't know if I'd even stay in Vegas. Then I met this guy. At first, he was cool. After a few long conversations, I realized we had so much in common, and I decided to work with him on a business level.

He was talented but had no support or direction, and I thought I had it all figured out. I had some experience and connections, and he wanted to be a rapper—but he was also an artist and an author. Everything I booked for my brand, I'd bring him along. We were everywhere together, and we were fucking, which made it feel even better. Looking back, maybe it wasn't a good idea to mix business and pleasure. He knew too much about me, and I think he started feeling himself, not valuing me the way he should.

Still, everyone was receptive to his brand, so I didn't mind taking a backseat. His people got involved, and I thought we had a great team. I remember writing a check for a ton of merchandise—for both his brand and mine—but mostly his. At the time, I didn't realize how crucial branding was. I thought all I needed to do was make my little swimwear line and help build his brand. I thought we were partners, but there was no contract, so really, I was just being naive.

Over time, I saw how he and his team started acting toward me. They would talk big shit about me and my struggles, disregard my ideas, and his mom—now his manager—was making all the decisions. They treated me like I hadn't built all of this from the ground up. I thought I was helping build an empire, something like Roc-A-Fella, but in reality, I was putting myself and my brand last. My brand was starting to fade.

I tried to keep things going, but it was never the same. My original models weren't around anymore, and the new ones I brought in just weren't the same. I felt stupid for not appreciating the work my first team had done. I was broke, getting evicted, squatting in homes, barely holding it together. I have to admit, that guy was still there through it all, but neither of us was the same. The fun was over.

Eventually, I slowed down helping him and focused on getting my brand back on track. Once I did, his brand started to fade. Years passed. He managed to keep some of his talents alive, but nothing came close to what I had done for him—and I didn't care. I needed my brand to win. I continued showcasing whenever I could, connected with a new, up-and-coming modeling agency in Vegas, and got busy keeping my brand alive. I'll always appreciate the owner of that agency. She gave me opportunities when I was down, and I was determined not to waste them.

But even with her support, I wasn't growing. I wasn't making money, just a few custom orders here and there. One day, she booked me for a show. I declined and told her I no longer wanted to do bars or club showcases—I would only do vending and larger shows. Gigs that actually brought in money. She got mad, even said some crazy stuff about how she "built my brand" and that nobody would know me if it weren't for her. I had to go into my archives and send her my whole resume just to prove a point. I had to shut that thought down because at that moment, she had me fucked up.

Just like that, I was back motivated to build my brand again. KYSS was in full effect. I started working on new pieces. I'm now off probation, no more legal issues and was booked for NYFW, connected with some of the best models in Vegas, and booked one of the top photographers here to shoot my new designs. And now... I'm opening my very first real storefront.

I was scared and discouraged for so many years after my first fall. I didn't feel motivated to keep KYSS alive. But I knew this had been my dream for a long time, and I refused to give up. People having me fucked up along the way just sharpened my focus. I no longer need to be under anyone. I'm a boss. This is my brand, my vision, and I worked my ass off to keep it together.

I was scared to open a storefront because of my lack of sales over the past few years. Yes, it's risky—but if I don't believe in my own brand, how can I expect anyone else to? Social media and online sales work for most people, but for me, I like the old-school approach. I like interacting with my customers in person, seeing their expressions when they try on my pieces. And I love it. I love being here, building something I've dreamed about for so long. I beat the odds and now making money doing what I love. Words can't even express how grateful I am at this moment—and I did it all by myself.

I named my store KYSS Collections because over the years, I expanded beyond swimwear. I started designing lingerie, cocktail dresses, activewear, and simple women's clothing. I wanted to bring it all together—a little woman's cave of my own. I want every woman who walks in to immediately feel sexy regardless of their shape. This is my dream, my labor, my love. And finally, it's real.

I'll never forget the day of my grand opening. The feeling was magical. The crazy part was that none of my so-called friends or family members showed up for me. It was just me and my kids—and that was okay.

Deeply Rooted

I was so proud to have accomplished something on my own. I stood there looking around the room, realizing that even without the crowd, the moment still mattered. I mattered. Everything I had been through, every tear, every setback, every doubt—I carried it all into that space with me and still opened those doors.

That day taught me something powerful: sometimes your support won't look like what you imagined. Sometimes the applause is quiet. Sometimes it's just your children watching you choose yourself. And sometimes that's enough to keep going.

I learned that showing up for myself was the real victory. I didn't need validation to know how far I had come. I had already survived things that should have broken me, and here I was—building, creating, standing on all Ten.

That grand opening wasn't just about a business. It was proof that I could start again. That I could believe in myself even when no one else did. That I could keep going, not for approval, but for my future—and for my kids who were watching me turn pain into purpose.

And that, to me, was everything.

Chapter Five

Fake Ass Marriage

Deeply Rooted

Funny how life works. After years of heartbreak, pain, fights, and struggle, we finally did it. We got married. And for one moment, I felt like I won. Like I finally had "A real relationship". Like I finally married my Best Friend.

But it wasn't the Fairytale i wanted, It was more like a setup.

We'd been together on and off for years before any of this even started. He always acted like we were "just business partners," but we both knew We were way more than that. And the worst part? I wasn't the one hiding him. He was the one hiding us the whole time. He was the one lying to other women about what we really had. He was the one pretending we weren't together although we were living together, sleeping together every night and more. For a while, he was my only emotional support, and he loved the hell out of my kids, so I convinced myself that I needed him. Looking back, I can admit i was stupid, desperate even to be dealing with a man who couldn't stop playing mind games and hid behind the act of being a "REAL NIGGA"

We got married in a chapel located in Downtown Las Vegas, the ceremony quick and quiet — just us. No family or friends. Just a piece of paper and a promise he didn't even know how to keep.

Because right after we left, he walked to a different car and drove off to be with another woman The one he was living with at the time after one of our temporary breakups. The one he said was a mistake for even messing with… *by constantly saying that he fucked up and only wanted me.*

Before we got married, we had just returned from another baecation in Miami. About a week later, we finally had a real, honest conversation—one of those moments where you sit back and reminisce about everything you've been through together. By that time, we had already lost the place we were living in, and honestly, neither one of us thought it was a good idea to get another place together. Our relationship was extremely toxic, and we both knew it. So, I got my own place, and he went off to play house with someone else.

I couldn't tell you what lies he was feeding her, and at the time, I didn't care.

Even though we weren't living together anymore, we were still together in every other way. We hung out daily. When I called him, he answered—EVERYTIME. It didn't matter where he was or who he was with. That alone made me believe I was the one who really mattered. I felt like I was the one he truly wanted to be with. The one he chose. The one he couldn't let go of.

So, I never worried about the other women. I never questioned my place. Now don't get me wrong i was sometimes irritated when he lied to me about a few of them, but overall, I believed that he showed me that I'll always come before any of them based on his availability and his consistency with me, and that was enough for me.

But that's how the illusion worked.

Because looking back now, I see it clearly. He wasn't choosing me—he was choosing access. He was choosing convenience. He was choosing to keep me emotionally tied while he lived a completely different reality elsewhere.

So yes, on our wedding night, I slept alone.

While I was laying there with the title of being his wife, he was laid up with someone else.

Deeply Rooted

That's the part that still doesn't sit right with me—not because I didn't know who he was, but because I convinced myself that what we had was real just because he never fully let me go.

And in that moment, I felt like shit, Worthless. Like I was right back where I started. Mad at myself for allowing this nigga to play me all over again...

He sold me some bullshit ass story about him needed time to end things with her and promised he was going to make things right with me. And I believed him — because I wanted to believe him so bad it hurt.

But days later, nothing changed. He still stayed with her. Still acted like we weren't married. Still treated me like I was the side bitch he could keep on the back burner.

And I was tired. I was done. I was over it.

I sent him messages telling him we made a mistake and that we needed to end it before we hated each other. Again, he promised me it would change. He promised me he was going to "make it right." And even though he kept selling the same dreams I kept believing them I mean I was Hella gone over this man.

Deeply Rooted

Then he came over one night after work, stayed for a little while, and left before it got late — because he had to get back home before she got there and I remember thinking to myself

What part of the game is this? Straight BULL SHIT

That was the moment I spazzed

I texted him moments after he left and let him have it, I was done. and I didn't give a fuck about what came out of my mouth i wanted him to feel every bit of it.

I was tired of being the side chick to the man I married.

He had the audacity to say, "You knew what it was before we got married."

At that moment, I lost it even more and was in rage.

So, I sent the other woman a copy of our marriage certificate.

I mean she needed to know and why the fuck was I hiding his secrets anyway?

Deeply Rooted

I wasn't even mad at her — Although she had an issue with me, but mostly all his women did. They would all talk shit about me via social media and I would never reciprocate then same energy because why should I?

They were NOT my problem, He was. I was mad at him.

I was mad at myself.

I was mad that I allowed myself to be in a position where I was fighting for a man who didn't even see me as a priority.

She kicked him out after that and a few days later he came to move in with me because he had nowhere else to go. I let him. Per usual, I thought things would be different. I thought we'd finally start the marriage he promised.

But it only lasted a few weeks.

Because she called, wanting him back. she didn't care he was married or any of that just like I didn't care about whatever they had, so I get it, Again, she didn't owe me anything, he did.

She just wanted what she wanted.

Deeply Rooted

We were both fighting for a man who wanted both of us at the same time. Lame as hell.

Eventually, it ended. Not because he changed — but because he filed for an annulment and I just didn't care about us being married anymore so I had started talking to other people. I was tired of the cycle.

the annulment didn't happen, and we ended up back together. on and off. We continued to stay married, but not in a way that mattered. Our relationship was really broken but neither one of us had the strength to really let go completely so after years of playing the same game, we decided to give it a real try…

.

Chapter Six

Contemplation

Fake ass Marriage Continues...

Deeply Rooted

Seven years later, I was still dealing with the same old bullshit. Still watching him lie. Still watching him cheat with any woman who crossed his path—including a few who once called themselves my friends.

I used to think he loved me because of how he showed up for my kids. He played the stepdad role well, and for a long time, I confused that with real love. But looking back, I see it for what it was—another form of manipulation. He was good at being a father when it benefited him. When it made him look good. When it kept me attached.

What he was never good at was consistency.

He never stayed long. Never settled. Never made us a priority. Every time he started getting close to another woman, he found a reason to leave. And somehow, the blame always landed on me. I was the problem. I wasn't being a good wife. Meanwhile, I was giving him everything I had— I was emptying myself trying to hold something together that he never intended to protect.

I remember one night clearly. He had been out all night. When he finally came home, he laid down next to me like nothing was wrong. No apology. No explanation. Nothing. Then, just before falling asleep, he told me he was leaving me.

just like that.

No conversation. No accountability. Just another exit, delivered quietly, like the shit was normal...

How are you supposed to feel when your husband tells you—right before going to bed—that he's leaving you?

Confused, right?

I know we'd been going through it. I know things weren't perfect. But after everything he put me through—the women, the drama, the lies, the family shit I never signed up for—*he* was the one walking away? This shit is wild bro.

From my perspective, strength is strength for a reason. Some people just aren't built to sit in the mess they created. I'm not "trying" to say that he's weak, but when you look at the pattern, the actions speak for themselves.

Thoughts become words, and words become actions. When you start thinking a man is

Deeply Rooted

cheating but you don't have proof, there are really only a few choices. Option one: you search. You start creeping on social media, scanning his phone, checking his clothes, reading into every move, every shift in energy. You do all that just to find exactly what you already felt was there. Because yes—women's intuition is real. But once you find it, now you're hurting in every way possible. Emotionally wrecked. Angry. Embarrassed. Spiraling.

Or there's option two. You leave it alone. You pray about it. You continue to live your life. And if the truth comes out—and it always does—then you decide whether to leave or work it out. Either way is hard, but in my opinion, option two lets you move with a clearer, stronger mindset and when the darkness finally comes to light, you're already focused on better. You already know your worth. You already know what you bring to the table. So if that person chooses to fuck it up, it's truly their loss.

Or… there's always that third unspoken option—where you just spazz the fuck out because he has you completely fucked up.

Choose wisely. It really does make a difference.

Deeply Rooted

And if I'm being honest, I've done ALL I've been that girl running through his shit, finding exactly what I was looking for, arguing with his other women, acting out in ways I'm not proud of. Acting out in front of people. Making a fool of myself. Reaching out to other men just to feel wanted, just to piss him off. And I can tell you right now—that way didn't work for me.

We were trying to really damage each other more. He wasn't having it, and neither was I. But I still stayed. And by staying, I hurt myself even more. Letting him go felt impossible. Forgiving him felt forced. Moving forward felt fake. We beefed daily—over what he put me through and over what I did in response. Neither one of us was willing to truly let it go, yet we kept sticking around through all the heartache.

Crazy shit, right?

To this very moment, I still don't fully understand us. And I'm starting to believe I never will. Even if we did love each other—love alone wouldn't be enough. We were too Toxic, Too Damaged.

Before that night I know he was cheating again. my spirit kept telling me. I didn't take all the

Deeply Rooted

steps to confirm it, but I can feel it in my soul. His demeanor has changed drastically. And after knowing this man—his habits, his patterns, his moods—I can tell when something isn't right. He's predictable, even if he doesn't realize it himself...

So when he said what he said, I wasn't really surprised—but it still hurt. I had seen this version of him before. I knew how this usually went. I was just hoping that this time, he had finally gotten all that weird shit out of his system.

I wanted to believe we were past it. That the lies were done. That the bouncing between women was over. That I didn't have to keep proving I was worth choosing.

But hope has a way of making you ignore patterns you already recognize.

I saw the same moves. The same energy. Just packaged a little differently—because now he had a new roster. Different names but same behavior. And as usual, I was getting the same results.

Deeply Rooted

Now here we go again. Another situation. Another woman he's playing with. Another reminder that nothing had really changed

She's been around for a minute—supposedly his friend's "cousin." Or some shit. He tells me he's only interested in doing music with her, but that's hard to believe considering he already told me she's been all over him, crushing on him for a minute. The night he admitted that just so happened to be the same night he didn't come home.

Now all of a sudden, she's everywhere. All over his social media. In his text messages. Having long, intimate conversations with him. And as usual, I'm the one tripping.

At this point, I'm calm—but not because I'm okay. I'm calm because I'm tired. I honestly don't have the strength anymore to fight with this man. But on the flip side… he still has me fucked up. Again.

And that's the part that hurts the most— knowing better, feeling it all, and still standing here trying to understand something that keeps breaking me.

Deeply Rooted

Because here's the truth nobody wants to say out loud:

this man hated me.
All the signs were there. They had been there for years—the lies, the cheating, the body shaming. Telling me I was fat and ugly while hyping the next woman up so she could feel better than me, prettier than me. He tried to break me every chance he got, telling me he didn't like me, that I'd never be the one for him because I was too flawed.

I purposely ignored all of it, hoping he would change.

They always say, *if you knew better, you'd do better*—and clearly, I didn't know a damn thing.

Hell, he even used to call me stupid. A part of me believed it, but I was always too cold to let it get to me.

Everything happens for a reason though. In a way, I feel like I needed to go through that. I needed to feel all of it, because now I know better—and there ain't no MF way I'll ever allow myself to be treated like that again by any man.

Deeply Rooted

It's just unfortunate that it took two failed, fucked-up marriages to realize my worth.

People would tell me I deserved better, that he wasn't shit—but it's hard to hear anyone when you're too far gone. Especially when you feel like they don't really fuck with you either. In my head, I thought they were just hating, jealous, or on some other shit. I wanted him to change so badly just to prove everyone wrong—but that shit never happened.

Truth is, they were all right.

What annoyed me the most was how he constantly had other women coming at me, attacking my character, when they didn't have a fucking clue. Like I was the reason for his behavior. Like I wasn't good enough for him—while he was out here betraying a "good nigga" image to them by exposing my flaws or feeding them lies, saying I was the one dogging him or cheating on him.

I believe they knew better than to believe that shit. They just didn't give a fuck. Or maybe they did believe him because he was decent to them. They didn't have to deal with his daily bullshit. So of course I looked like the messed-up one.

Deeply Rooted

But you'd think they'd at least acknowledge the fact that he was unfaithful and mistreating the woman he married. That alone speaks volumes about his character. Instead, some of these women wanted the same shit I wanted—to protect him, love him, and hope he'd become the man they needed.

Some got him in small increments. Some got him in moments of physical pleasure. But none of us truly mattered.

He didn't give a fuck about anything.

He was broken and didn't even love himself. The sad part is, he didn't realize he had a problem. So instead of taking accountability, he made excuses for his actions.

Can't nobody say I wasn't holding down my wifey duties—because I did **everything** for that man. They can miss me with that bullshit. No matter what I did, he was still unhappy with me.

So to all the women who thought I was the problem—girl, BYE.

I don't wish this kind of pain on anyone. But if you come for a woman over a man, enabling his lame ass behavior, dogging his own wife,

Deeply Rooted

repeatedly abandoning his family, and airing out personal business for entertainment—you are part of the problem, babe.

And I pray you seek healing…

But I'm learning something painful and ugly:

The more you give, the more they take.
The more you love, the more they use.
The more you try to fix them, the more broken you become.

And the crazy part is, He's not even trying to be better.

So yeah—he tells me he's leaving, and I'm confused. But I'm not surprised.

Because this has been the pattern from the beginning. The cycle of love, manipulation, guilt, and pain. The constant reminder that I'm not enough unless I'm hurting and a constant reminder that this has been FAKE ASS MARRIAGE from the beginning.

Deeply Rooted

Chapter Seven

Scared and Lonely

Deeply Rooted

At times, I sit and really think to myself—

what is family for real? I understand that I have blood relatives, but I don't feel like I have a real family. My so-called family is always full of drama and bullshit, and it seems like the only time we're able to come together—or pretend to like one another—is when there's some sort of event: a funeral, a birthday party, a wedding etc... Other than that, it's all fucking drama.

I separated myself from most of my family years ago because I can't get down with certain shit. I didn't like how judgmental or envious they could be toward one another for one and i hate that most of the women in my family are so forgiving toward outsiders who betray them over shit that's plain unforgivable yet will turn their backs on their own flesh and blood over simple shit. That part never sat right with me.

I've had mommy and daddy issues most of my life and at times I really do feel parentless. Yes, my parents are still living, but it feels like I don't have any parents at all. I have an aunt who have always supported me if I really needed it, but sometimes she can be messy also so I try to limit that interaction when I can. I use to think that me and my sisters would always be close but then again it be weird shit going on with them also. Leaving me to think that all I need is my babies.

My kids are everything to me. Even when I'm frustrated, overwhelmed, and exhausted, I still love being a mom. They keep me going. They give me purpose when everything else feels like it's falling apart.

My spouse isn't really shit right now, which is why we filed for yet another divorce, But today, I'm really feeling a way because I'm being forced to move out of my home, and I can't help but think to myself, *nobody can even help me when I really need them.* My aunt offered to help financially, but today I'm not okay mentally. I'm sad. I'm depressed. I'm scared. I'm literally slipping and can't get up.

For the past week, one of my aunts has been texting me, asking for updates and wanting to know what my plans are. I guess that's her way of telling me to stop crying over things I can't control and to come up with a plan. I get it—I do—but I don't have the mental strength right now to pull myself together. I turned this house into a home. I was finally stable—more stable than I've ever been in my entire life—and now I feel like it's all being snatched away from me.

Deeply Rooted

I'm losing control, and it's over the weakest shit.

Not because I couldn't cover my rent—but because of a lame-ass dude and a stupid ass divorce. On top of that, I had just opened my storefront. I finally did something for myself, and now everything feels like it's collapsing all at once.

Another aunt checks in on me from time to time, but honestly, I don't know what to tell them. I'm fucking drowning, and I don't have a clue what to do. Unfortunately, I can't just leave. I'm facing yet another charge over some stupid shit. It's clearly retaliation but the courts will still find some sort of loophole to destroy us even more., I'm now locked into a commercial lease for the next three years. But truthfully, I wish I could escape and never return.

There's so much running through my head that I never know what to say to the few people who claim they want to help. As for everyone else, I feel like they only reach out to be nosy or messy—not out of genuine concern. I've been pretty open about my situation, so I'm sure my entire family knows what's going on. But this is what they do—they gossip.

Deeply Rooted

Yesterday, I was so lost that I reached out to anyone who would answer, on some desperate shit, even though I knew deep down they didn't really give a damn. Now I've exposed all of my current drama, and I regret it.

When I talk to my mom, she ends the conversation on some bullshit or rushes to hang up. One thing about my mom—she doesn't like to talk long if it doesn't benefit her in some way. Right now, her main concern is going on vacation, so me and my girls possibly being homeless is the least of her worries. I get it, though. In a way, I put myself in this situation by messing with a fucking loser. That's the truth. But I'm still sad.

My sisters keep telling me to sell all my shit, while at the same time bragging about the trips they have planned. That shit annoyed the fuck out of me. I kept thinking, *fuck that trip—I'm about to lose everything I worked for,* and the only advice they have is to sell all my shit and start over. Like, bitch, I worked my ass off for this. Fuck that.

Because of my past choices, I've already had to start over so many times. I'm tired of starting over. But also, part of me feels like my sisters was never too fond of me or my

Deeply Rooted

accomplishments so of course i took that comment in a whole different way. I understand it's nobody's responsibility to save me, but telling someone to sell everything and give up on their dreams—especially when they were never truly happy for me in the first place—is wild. I feel like me giving up on everything I've built is exactly what they want, and that shit is not an option.

And let's be real—these are the same sisters who still praise our dad, the man who raped me as a child, and somehow still speak his name with honor. So no, I wasn't hearing anything they had to say.

Maybe I'm just mad. Maybe I'm mad at the whole world. Maybe I am the problem. Maybe I am tripping. But so, what? I had my hopes up for a minute, thinking I had people / Family that would have my back. Silly me to believe that shit anyway. People are who they are, and the colors was shown many years ago. I guess I was thinking just maybe some thig would be different. The crazy part is that I really didn't want much from anyone other than some sort of emotional support but even that was too much to ask.

Deeply Rooted

I have a cousin who keeps reaching out, but I'm starting to believe she just wants something to judge and gossip about with her sister. Like for one Why do you keep bringing her up in every conversation, telling me what she's saying about my situation, when she doesn't even fuck with me or the family? How could she understand something she's never had to live through? And giving opinions about a person or situation you don't fuck with is weird to me so they both can go find something else to do and leave me the fuck alone.

Then there's my ex. This dude has the audacity to be reaching out but only when it's convenient for him, like when he wants something or wants to see if he still has access to me. He would call me just to brag about other hoes and tries to make it seem like all of this is my fault because I went through his phone. Saying stupid shit like if I had just minded my business, I wouldn't be in this predicament. He's weak ass fuck to me. He just wants his ego boosted. I'll let the court handle his ass. Fucking narcissist…

Meanwhile, it's just me and my two daughters. My son decided to up move out right after my husband left, and that shit hit me by surprise because I wanted so much more for him. But he wanted to be closer to a family that was never there for him. That shit hurt on a different level. Maybe me being the strict parent pushed him toward his dad's side of the family because It's easier there—they don't push him to finish school or build a future. But he's an adult now, and he made his choice. Mama will always be here if he needs me, but I must allow him to experience life and trust that I did good with raising him the best I could. He's been through a lot also, witnessing me being both physically and mentally abused so I kind of get it... He needs something new, a different environment.

Today, my daughter had to walk home from school for the first time because I had court and couldn't pick her up. I don't know why, but that shit crushed me. I was worried out of my mind. Yes, I'm the mom who still drop my girls off and pick them up every day—shit is crazy outside.

Things are bad for me right now mentally and emotionally. I want to break so bad. I don't know how I was going to make it through each day—but I am trying, and I refuse to give up on life. Side note: Court ended. My girls are home safe. I'm back at my shop. Yet I still feel empty and alone. I'm afraid daily. But every morning, somehow, I find the strength to keep going.

Deeply Rooted

Trusting the process and trusting God's timing. Maybe it's a good thing I stopped including people in my plans, stopped giving them so much access to my life. Sometimes that shit only brings you down further. You expect more from people, hoping this time you'll be saved—when the truth is, you must save yourself.

I appreciate the people I do have, but I still feel alone. I feel like I need to limit what I share because I need to protect myself from disappointment. That alone makes me feel alone. I'm not always sure I can pick myself up every time I am breaking down. There are moments I even question my faith and make desperate decisions.

Moving forward, I want to do better. I want to feel better. I just don't know where to begin. My history and lack of genuine support made me naïve. Who can I really trust?

I'm scared—especially for my daughters. I feel lonely as fuck. When I ask myself who I can run to when I just need love, the answer right now is no one. And that is not a good feeling to live with.

Deeply Rooted

Scared and Lonely

I am tired of being strong in silence,
of swallowing pain so my children can breathe.
Tired of asking for help
and being handed judgment instead.

I don't need saving—
I need understanding.
I don't need lectures—
I need love.

Some nights, courage looks like staying alive.
Some mornings, faith is just getting out of bed.
And if all I have is myself today,
then I will learn how to be enough.

Chapter Eight

Stability

Deeply Rooted

To most people, it looks like I have it all together.
I don't.
I'm just trying to figure it out like everybody else. Looks can be deceiving.

I've learned how to hold myself a certain way in public. How to smile through exhaustion. How to speak with confidence even when my stomach is tight with worry. People assume I'm strong because I don't fall apart in front of them. They assume I'm good because I don't ask for much help. But what they don't see is how hard I work just to stay afloat—to remain stable in a world that's never really given me a solid foundation.

A lot of people feel intimidated by me. They think they have to be on a certain level to be around me. I guess because I like nice things, because I carry myself with pride, because I've always had expensive taste even when my pockets didn't match it. And yes, I bust my ass to have what I have. But what people don't understand is that liking nice things doesn't mean life is nice to me. It doesn't mean I'm not struggling. It doesn't mean I'm not constantly one step away from everything falling apart.

Deeply Rooted

Growing up, we moved a lot. Stability was never something I experienced—it was something I watched other people have. I never knew what it felt like to stay in one place long enough to feel safe. Long enough to exhale. Long enough to trust that tomorrow would look like today. For most of my life, instability felt normal. Chaos felt familiar. Surviving became a skill instead of a season.

Now I'm a mother, trying to give my children what I never had. And that pressure is heavy. Being a single mom means there's no room to fall apart. No safety net. No backup plan. Every decision I make affects my kids. Every mistake costs more than just my pride. I'm constantly trying to do the right thing—stay out of trouble, keep my record clean, stay focused, stay working, stay legal, stay sane. But it's hard when you're doing it alone.

I don't have a village.
No consistent help.
No one saying, "I got the kids, go breathe."
No one checking in daily to see if I'm okay.

It's just me—navigating court dates, bills, school schedules, emotional breakdowns, and healing—all at the same time. I don't have the luxury of spiraling. I don't get to sit in my pain

Deeply Rooted

for too long. I still have to show up, even when my heart is heavy and my mind feels crowded.

The past few months have tested me in ways I didn't think I'd survive. I've been lost—questioning everything. Who I can trust. Who actually cares. Whether or not I'm strong enough to make it through this without losing myself. February 26, 2024, is the day my partner walked out on me after I went through his phone and found him cheating. He tried to flip it like I was wrong for checking his phone, using that as his excuse to leave. But the truth is, he's just a weak man who can't take accountability. He runs from his mess and leaves destruction behind.

It's been like that for years. And I hate admitting this—but I kept allowing him back. Over and over again. Hoping things would change. Hoping love would be enough. Hoping stability could grow out of dysfunction.

Today is April 27, 2024, and I'm tired in a way that feels final. Not dramatic. Not emotional. Just done. For the first time, I couldn't even cry. I felt numb. Detached. All the material things I once held onto out of fear—I'm letting go of them now. Selling them. Releasing them. Because none of it is worth this pain.

Deeply Rooted

He sent me $500 with a note that said, *"leave me tf alone."* The disrespect was loud. And what's crazy is that $500 doesn't even touch the damage. Remind you, I now have to move because he told the landlord he's no longer living in the home, which triggered them to want me out too because part of reason for us being approved for the home in the first place was due to our stability as a two-income household... I'm packing my life up once again because of a man's decisions—not because I failed, but because I trusted the wrong person.

That money doesn't compare to the emotional abuse, the instability, the embarrassment, the stress, the sleepless nights, or the fear my kids have had to feel. What I really need from him—peace, accountability, protection—he can't give. So I'm choosing myself.

Lately, I've been questioning my faith. Wondering why God keeps allowing me to feel this kind of pain. Why I can't seem to catch a break. Why every time I build something, it feels like it's ripped away. But I'm starting to understand that some blessings can't reach me because of who I keep around. Some doors won't open if the wrong people still have access to my life. Letting go feels scary—but staying stuck feels worse.

Deeply Rooted

As a child, I was always afraid to leave situations that were hurting me—but I left anyway. I learned how to survive early. I even tattooed the word *faith* on my foot because I've been walking by faith my whole life. And if faith carried me through then, it has to carry me now.

I don't know exactly how I'm going to make it through this season. I just know I have to. For my kids. For myself. For the woman I'm becoming. I am worthy of stability. I am worthy of peace. I am worthy of a life that doesn't feel like a constant emergency.

I will no longer allow a man to have power over my peace. I will no longer stay in situations that drain me emotionally and spiritually. This is my first step toward healing—recognizing that this life no longer serves me.

So I choose peace.
I choose real love.
I choose stability—even if I have to build it alone.

I know it won't be easy. I know there will be days I feel scared and overwhelmed. But I also know God didn't bring me this far just to leave me here.

Chapter Nine
Jealousy in Disguise

Deeply Rooted

Am I the Problem?

Sometimes I sit alone and really ask myself the hardest questions.
Am I the problem?
Am I the reason I have no real friends?
Am I the reason I lack support?
Am I the reason my relationships failed?
Am I the reason my kids act the way they do, or why my finances never seem stable?

I've always said *God don't like ugly*, but lately I've caught myself wondering—am I the ugly that God doesn't like?

I truly try to be a decent human being. I know I have flaws—everyone does. I can be aggressive at times, but usually only when my feelings are hurt or when I feel played with emotionally. Outside of that, I believe I'm kind, outgoing, loyal, and genuine. But maybe that's part of the problem. Maybe I'm too nice. Maybe people get used to my softness, my patience, my understanding—and the moment I set a boundary or say no, they disappear.

It's like the first time I choose myself, everyone backs away.

I know my kids are spoiled. I won't deny that. Sometimes I feel like I waited too long to

Deeply Rooted

discipline them properly, and now I'm paying for it. At times they seem ungrateful, entitled, even out of control. And that hurts because everything I did was out of love. I thought protecting their happiness would protect their hearts—especially when people kept leaving us. Maybe instead of preparing them for the world, I tried too hard to shield them from it.

The lack of support I experience feels deeper than coincidence. A lot of it feels rooted in envy, hate, or misinformation. Stories told about me. Assumptions made without my side ever being heard. Some people I probably did push away. Others never liked me to begin with. And some people simply don't want to see you doing better than them. They'll clap for you—as long as you don't outgrow them.

That part is painful, but it's real.

So sometimes I wonder if I am the problem, because I don't understand why so much bullshit keeps happening to me. Why people are so cold. Why support feels conditional. I know I've ruined some relationships if I'm being honest, so maybe this is karma. We all fail to appreciate good people sometimes. We don't always know how to keep them around.

Deeply Rooted

Especially when we have deeply rooted issues that we still are learning how to heal from.

But I also believe this—some people don't deserve access to us.

And maybe that belief comes from survival, not arrogance.

My husband, for example. He genuinely believes I should appreciate him simply because he's around—because he chose to be with a woman who already had children. He minimizes everything I do. Cooking. Cleaning. Working. Managing businesses. Holding the household together. He says I do those things because I'm a mother, not because I'm a wife.

What he doesn't understand is that I do it for the household—for everyone.

My kids are older now. They're in their own world. I will always be their mother—no matter what—but my role as a wife still matters. I carry responsibilities that should never fall on one person alone. A man shouldn't reduce his role in a household just because the woman has children. But instead of stepping up, he tears me down.

Deeply Rooted

And when things go wrong—whether in our home, my friendships, or my family—he blames me. Says I'm the reason people leave. Says I'm difficult. Says I push everyone away. And for a long time, I believed him. I cried myself to sleep praying to be a better wife, a better mother, a better sister, a better daughter, a better friend.

But then I started to look around.

Besides my children and my sister, everyone else has hurt me in some way. Disappointed me. Betrayed me. So how am I always the problem?

I used to think that when people show you who they are, you let them go. And I still believe that. But loneliness has a way of making you forgive things you shouldn't. It makes you keep people around who continuously hurt you just so you don't feel alone.

That's where I take accountability.

Not because I wronged people but because I kept allowing people to wrong me.

I ignored red flags. I numbed myself. I stayed quiet when I should have spoken up. I stayed when I should have left. In my marriage, I endured so much pain that instead of walking away, I stooped to childish behavior and revenge. That wasn't strength that was exhaustion.

At the end of the day, we can blame everyone who hurt us, but the real damage happens when we allow it to continue.

Sometimes the strongest thing you can do is give it to God and let it go. Let Him remove the wrong people. Let Him make room for the right ones. Let Him heal the parts of you that keep confusing love with tolerance.

We all have room for improvement. Every single one of us.

And maybe the real problem isn't that I'm broken.
Maybe it's that I stayed too long in places that required me to shrink.

So again, Many times I ask myself if people really dislike me or if it's jealousy.

Truth is, it could be both.

Deeply Rooted

Jealousy is just another form of hate dressed up in a quieter outfit. It doesn't always come loud or obvious. Sometimes it comes smiling. Sometimes it comes clapping for you in public but whispering doubts behind closed doors. Sometimes it comes disguised as advice, concern, or love. And it took me a long time to learn that just because someone is close to you doesn't mean they're for you.

It's beneficial - necessary even to pay attention to who actually shows up for you. Not who watches you. Not who studies you. Not who hovers. Who shows up.

A lot of people will pretend to like you, but in reality, they don't. They'll stay around just close enough to observe your every move. They'll listen carefully, ask questions, and even offer insight on what they think you *should* do in certain situations. And on the surface, that sounds like support. But you have to watch that shit because everyone doesn't have your best interest at heart.

Some advice is intentional sabotage.

Some advice is meant to slow you down, confuse you, or plant doubt right when you're gaining momentum. Some people don't want to see you win. They don't want to see you do better than them. And instead of being honest about their insecurity, they mask it as "real talk" or "keeping it real."

Other times, people will call themselves your friend while quietly dissecting your every move just so they can copy you later and try to do it better. That's not friendship. That's competition disguised as connection. That's someone forming competitive energy instead of building partnership. And I've learned that some people don't want to grow *with* you they want to grow *past* you.

Most people don't believe in team building, and that's always been a problem for me. Because I don't see competition. I see collaboration. I give out free game because I genuinely want everybody to win. I don't believe success is limited. I don't believe someone else shining dims my light. But unfortunately, that energy is rarely reciprocated.

And when I ask myself if I'm the problem the real answer is yes. But not in the way people assume.

I love hard. I give deeply. I show up fully. But I can also be a monster when pushed.

Deeply Rooted

Hell, I'm a Gemini. I'm the best of both sides. I move with love first, always. Everything I do comes from love until I'm provoked, disrespected, or made to feel small for shining. And when that happens, I protect myself fiercely.

Jealousy in family hits different.

Sometimes it's relatives who watched you struggle, survive, and rise and instead of being proud, they resent you for it. They remind you of who you *used* to be every time you try to evolve. They minimize your growth, question your choices, or act like your healing makes you "different." And it does but different doesn't mean wrong.

Family jealousy often shows up as guilt. As obligation. As "don't forget where you came from." But what they really mean is, *don't go somewhere I couldn't.*

Jealousy in friendships is quieter but deadlier.

It looks like friends who stop clapping when your wins get bigger. Friends who don't celebrate your milestones. Friends who only call when they need something but disappear when you need support. Friends who slowly start distancing themselves once you outgrow the version of yourself they were comfortable with.

And then there's jealousy in relationships the most confusing disguise of all.

With my husband, I couldn't identify what the real issue was for a long time. I thought maybe it was jealousy. Hell, at times it felt like his entire family was jealous of me. But when it came to him, I realized it was something deeper.

He wanted me to focus on *him*. On *his* goals. On *his* dreams.

The moment I did something for myself, my career, my growth, my healing he hated that shit. It created friction. He would sabotage the peace, start arguments, or label me as selfish or not being a good person. And the crazy part? I started believing it.

Now that I'm thinking about it more clearly, that shit was strange.

Love doesn't shrink you. Love doesn't punish you for evolving. Love doesn't compete with you. Love doesn't resent your ambition. And love damn sure doesn't require you to abandon yourself to keep someone else comfortable.

Deeply Rooted

Jealousy in disguise will make you question yourself. It will make you dim your light. It will convince you that your growth is the problem when really, it's the trigger.

And the hardest truth I've had to face is this: Some people only love you when you're small. When you're struggling. When you're dependent. When your shine doesn't remind them of what they're avoiding in themselves.

But I'm no longer interested in shrinking.

I'm learning to discern energy. To listen to patterns instead of words. To trust my intuition even when it hurts. And to understand that not everyone who smiles at me is rooting for me.

Jealousy doesn't always come as hate. Sometimes it comes as love with conditions.

And I'm done accepting that shit

Deeply Rooted

Chapter Ten

I Thought He Loved Me —

Deeply Rooted

We've all felt that feeling we believe is love.

When I got married for the first time, I honestly wasn't sure if it was love. I think we were just doing what we felt was right at the time because we had a baby together. Don't get me wrong—I did have love for him, but I don't think I was ever *in love* with him. It felt more like obligation than romance more survival than passion.

After my first marriage ended, I thought I had finally found my Mr. Right.

When we first met, he felt like a breath of fresh air. He seemed different. Safer. More understanding. Things were good in the beginning until they weren't. Months later, he showed me who he really was.

Throughout our years together, I bent over backwards for him. I sacrificed my own happiness to make sure he was okay. I put his needs before my own, thinking that love meant selflessness even when it cost me everything. But maybe that was the problem. I stayed loyal to someone who didn't deserve it. I loved someone who never truly chose me.

I know I'm flawed shit we all are in some way —but damn.

Deeply Rooted

I opened myself up to him in ways I never had before. I told him my life story. My pain. My trauma. My fears. I did that hoping he would understand me and treat me differently than the men before him. I hoped he would be patient with my bad days, that he wouldn't take my struggles personally. I hoped he would want to help me heal not add to the damage.

Instead, he listened to my cries and made me cry harder.
He heard my pain and deepened my scars.
When I needed love the most, he became the most hurtful.

Every time I thought it couldn't get worse, it did.

Now, he feels completely heartless. Like I don't matter at all. In the beginning, he sold me a dream. He played his role well. I was blind. But now I see everything clearly. I thought he loved me. I'm realizing now that he never did…

Deeply Rooted

Release and Letting Go

Today, I woke up wanting to talk to him about our last encounter. I wanted to express how his behavior has been affecting me; how distant and careless he's been. But when I called him, it was clear he didn't care. And honestly, he hasn't cared for a long time.

I wanted to save my marriage. I wanted to save the friendship I thought we had. I was naive. I ignored every sign that screamed he didn't want me.

Throughout the years, he cheated repeatedly. He treated other women better than he ever treated me as if I were the side chick. Yes, we lived together. Yes, we were married. But none of that meant anything to him. He wasn't happy with himself, let alone with me. He had been crashing long before I realized it, and I thought I could save him.

I thought love meant staying.
I thought loyalty meant endurance.
I thought if I loved him hard enough, we would survive.

But that wasn't reality.

Deeply Rooted

I was foolish and deeply lost in my emotions. I ignored the embarrassment, the humiliation, and how his actions were slowly destroying my self-worth. I didn't want to live without him. I thought I needed him. But one thing I refused to do was beg or compete for love.

The truth is simple—he just doesn't love me.

I've felt this realization before, but every time I got close to walking away, he would pull me back in. He would reach out to the kids, make them feel safe, tell them he loved them and would always be there. That softened me. That weakened me. But even that was manipulation. It was just his way of regaining access to me when he felt me slipping away.

Today, I am officially tired.

I can't hurt anymore.

I loved him with everything I had. Through cheating. Through disrespect. Through disappointment. Through broken promises. But I can't keep losing myself over someone who never truly valued me. I loved him more than I loved myself and that realization hurts more than anything he ever did.

Deeply Rooted

My family have been telling me this for years, but when you're deeply attached to someone, you ignore the truth. You lie to yourself. You convince yourself that one day they'll change. That one day they'll love you the way you deserve.

It felt like working endlessly toward something I believed would eventually pay off. But relationships don't work like that. You don't always get what you give. Sometimes, you give everything and still walk away empty.

They say you can't truly love someone if you don't love yourself. And that's true. He couldn't love me because he doesn't love himself. And I couldn't love him properly because I wasn't loving myself either.

We were bonded by trauma, not love. Sharing pain doesn't equal partnership. We never should have gotten married it only made the wounds deeper.

As I write this, I'm scared I'll never love someone the way I loved him. But maybe I will. And maybe next time, it'll be with someone who loves me back just as deeply.

I know love exists—but first, I need to find myself again.

Deeply Rooted

Today, the pain stops.

Letting go is hard. We've been together for so long. I'm used to him. The loneliness is real. But holding on is costing me more than letting go ever could.

It's time to release the pain.
It's time to choose peace.
It's time to redirect my energy into healing and self-love.

I love you—but I can't do this anymore.
I love you—but you don't love me the same.

And for that reason, I'm letting go—for real this time.

Let's both be free.

Deeply Rooted

Deeply Rooted

Praying for Peace

God,
I come to You tired.
Not just tired in my body but tired in my spirit.

I'm tired of loving people who hurt me.
Tired of carrying pain that was never meant to be mine.
Tired of begging for love that should have been given freely.

Today, I ask You for peace.
The kind of peace that doesn't need explanation.
The kind that settles my heart when my mind won't slow down.
The kind that reminds me I am safe—even when everything feels uncertain.

Deeply Rooted

Please help me release what no longer serves me.
Release the guilt.
Release the shame.
Release the memories that keep replaying in my head.
Release the version of myself that thought pain was love.

Cover my heart as I learn how to let go.
Heal the parts of me that stayed too long.
Restore the parts of me that were lost while trying to save someone else.

Protect my children.
Surround them with love, stability, and guidance.
Let them feel my strength—even on the days I feel weak.

Teach me how to love myself the way I tried to love others.
Give me discernment moving forward.

Deeply Rooted

Remove people from my life who come with chaos, confusion, or harm.
And replace them with peace, honesty, and genuine care.

When I feel lonely, remind me that I am never alone.
When I feel broken, remind me that You are still working on me.
When I feel afraid, remind me that I have survived worse—and I am still here.

I trust You with my healing.
I trust You with my future.
I trust You with my heart.

And from this day forward, I choose peace.
Even when it's uncomfortable.
Even when it's lonely.
Even when it requires letting go.

Amen.

Deeply Rooted

Chapter Eleven

Over It – Crash out Session

Deeply Rooted

Niggas really refuse to take accountability for *anything*.

This mf really had the audacity to say that I put myself and my kids in this situation—like he forgot what actually went down. Bitch ass nigga, did you forget that I had to move because **YOU** called the landlord? Probability lied about some hit and got me put out. It wasn't even about the rent anymore. You didn't want me in that house anymore to break me.

The same with the Jag and the Benz.

You're a piece of shit, and so is anyone else who thinks I caused this.

I went through your phone because you're a liar—and a drunk. You can't stay sober to save your own life. The truth is, you didn't leave because I went through your shit. You left because you're a coward. You can't face real problems. You run every time things get uncomfortable. You're a clown. And realizing that I was really chasing after your sorry ass makes me even more sick with myself.

If I'm to blame for anything, it's believing you would ever change. That's it.
FOH.

Deeply Rooted

And all these other bitches thinking they won baby, you didn't win *shit*. That boy ain't shit. It might feel cute right now, but one day you'll see. He doesn't respect his mom. He doesn't respect himself. And a man like that will **never** truly respect a woman.

Yeah, it took me a while—but I'm clear now. I'm over all the bullshit. And once a woman is fed up, it's a wrap.

Let's be honest niggas are ungrateful.

This nigga had a weak ass life before I came into the picture. And yeah, my life wasn't perfect either—but I was making moves while he was still talking about what he *"wanted* "to do. He had NO Motion… From the moment I met him, I went hard for him. I supported his dreams, his visions, his goals—so much that I set my own shit aside to focus on his.

That was stupid, but I didn't know any better back then.

I jeopardized my own freedom helping to promote his brand. I should've known right there that this nigga wasn't shit. It was obvious he was only fucking with me because I was making things happen. Over the years, I showed this man a good life—nice cars, nice

Deeply Rooted

places to live, vacations, excursions, shopping sprees, fine dining—all of it. He contributed some, but not even close to what I did. Most of that was *me*. I paid. I planned. I provided.

All ME -ME Bitch…

Now that I'm struggling, this nigga has the nerve to tell me to stop begging and get off my ass.

I'm honestly in shock—but not surprised. It just confirms everything I've already been thinking and saying about him. So yeah, I'm good. I always land on my feet. But this ungrateful nigga really got me fucked up.

And he keeps popping off about this court shit like I'm obsessed with it. But here's the reality—regardless of what I'm working on, regardless of how much money I'm bringing in, why the fuck should he just walk scot-free?

He turned my entire household upside down, left me in Hella debt and seems perfectly satisfied with the damage. Or maybe he's just too drunk to fully realize what he's done. Either way, as of today, he's making more money than I am—so why wouldn't I hold him accountable?

I may have been a fool over him for years—but not this time.

BITCH ASS NIGGA

Deeply Rooted

Deeply Rooted

Funny Business

Shit's funny how the wind blows.
Shit's funny how the same bullshit
just keeps going and growing,
and I still couldn't find the strength to let go.

We tried too many times.
Told too many lies.
Said we were done,
but never really cut them damn ties.

For a minute, I really thought we were forever.
All the red flags we hid,
all the shit we ignored.
Through it all, I really believed
you'd always be by my side.

Joke's on me.
Maybe I was too big of a prize
for someone who never deserved me.

Deeply Rooted

I should've never let you touch my body.
Never let you feel my curves.
Never gave you the access to shit you didn't deserve.
just to dog me the way you did.
I should've ended this a long time ago.

Shit's funny how love goes.
No matter how toxic someone is,
no matter how damaging they are to your soul,
you still let them stay in control
because letting go feels harder than staying.

But not today.
Not anymore.

Today I'm closing doors,
letting all that old shit go.
Whatever happens from here on out,
just know this is the road

you chose

Deeply Rooted

Now, I don't give a fuck about you
or your goals.

Now you mad—
but for what?
After you left me standing on my own,
ten toes down,
alone.

That shit was wack.
So no, there's no coming back.
You wanted your hoe, right?
Go deal with that.

Crash out if you want to.
That's no longer my concern.
I'm standing firm—
there will be no returns.

Not over here.

Deeply Rooted

You crazy as hell.
I got the power now,
and I'm cool.

So fuck what you going through.
Fuck what you heard.
Fuck all your excuses
for why you couldn't be a good man.
And fuck your trauma—
because I don't have to hold that shit
anymore.

I held it alone long enough.

That trauma bond is a motherfucker.
It makes you think you found your person,
your home,
your forever—
when that shit was never real.

You played me.
Now you deal with it on your own.

Deeply Rooted

I'm officially gone.
So leave me alone—
like you been telling everybody else anyway.

You made it seem like I was always the problem
for loving you.
Nigga, you crazy.

But it's cool.
Now it's time for us both to move on
and grow.

It don't make it hurt less.
But that's just the way life goes.

Deeply Rooted

Chapter Twelve

Imperfections

Deeply Rooted

Nobody's perfect. Not me, not you, not anyone. And yet, we often live as if we must be. We strive to appear flawless—flawless in love, flawless in work, flawless in parenting, flawless in our friendships, and flawless in the way the world perceives us. The truth is, perfection is an illusion, a societal mirage that leaves most of us exhausted, frustrated, and often disappointed in ourselves.

I've spent much of my life trying to be perfect. To get it right. To balance it all. motherhood, relationships, work, friendships, responsibilities, and self-care without faltering. And I've failed. Not in small ways, but in ways that shook me to my core. And that's okay. Because imperfection is where growth lives. Imperfection is where learning begins. Imperfection is proof that you are human.

My pride has put me in some challenging positions. I've made decisions that weren't always wise, choices that led to heartache, financial setbacks, or burned bridges. Yet every time, I emerged stronger. Every time, I learned something about myself, about others, about life. The cost of imperfection is steep at times, but the reward resilience, wisdom, and self-awareness is priceless.

Deeply Rooted

My love life has always been messy. I've lost friends over relationships, sacrificed myself for people who didn't deserve my devotion, and allowed heartbreak to motivate me in ways I didn't always understand. I sometimes feed off pain because it drives me to prove I am more than my circumstances. It pushes me to work harder, to strive for stability, to create the life I envision. But it's also taught me a valuable lesson: seeking perfection in love or in others is a trap. People are flawed. Love is messy. And happiness isn't found in someone else's approval; it's found in embracing your own imperfections.

Being a parent amplifies this lesson. My children need me to embrace imperfection, to show them that mistakes are part of life, that failure is not final, and that strength comes from getting up when life knocks you down. I refuse to let my flawed decisions harm them. But I'm honest about it I don't always get it right. Sometimes, my choices pull me away from them. Sometimes, I choose the path that seems best in the moment but has consequences I can't yet see. Even so, I go hard for the people I love, even when that means risking my comfort, my peace, or my safety. Imperfection doesn't excuse carelessness, but it does allow for humanity.

Deeply Rooted

I've often sacrificed stability to help others. I'd come into a good lump of cash, and instead of investing in my future, I spent it showing love, generosity, or loyalty—sometimes to people who didn't deserve it. I've learned the hard way that giving should not come at the cost of your foundation. Giving is beautiful, but giving recklessly is dangerous. The lesson here is not that generosity is bad, but that boundaries are essential. Imperfection includes knowing where to say "no" without guilt. Imperfection includes learning to prioritize yourself even when others expect everything from you.

I've tried to be perfect in friendships too. I've been there for people when it was inconvenient. I've planned events, offered support, lent money, and given my time freely. And yes, sometimes I expected gratitude in return. That's human. But I've learned that perfection in others' eyes is fleeting people will leave when it's hard, when it costs them, when your shine outshines theirs. Imperfection is learning to accept that not everyone will appreciate or reciprocate. Your value is not measured by how others treat you; it's measured by how faithfully you live according to your own integrity.

Education on imperfection is vital. Life doesn't hand out perfection, and the more we chase it, the more we suffer. Research shows that striving for perfectionism wanting to be flawless in every domain leads to stress, anxiety, and burnout. Psychologists even distinguish between adaptive perfectionism, which motivates growth, and maladaptive perfectionism, which punishes yourself for perceived failures. I've lived in both spaces. I've tried to be perfect at work, perfect in relationships, perfect as a parent, perfect in my home, perfect in my friendships, and perfect in self-presentation. And the truth is, I failed. I've failed a lot. And I've learned that failure is not the enemy, it's the teacher.

I also realize that imperfection is liberating. When I accept that I am flawed, that I will make mistakes, that I cannot control everything or everyone, I can finally breathe. I can finally let go of shame, fear, and resentment. I can finally invest in myself without guilt. I can finally teach my children that they don't have to be flawless to be loved, to be respected, or to succeed. That lesson alone is worth the struggle of imperfection.

I am flawed. I make mistakes. I misstep. I hurt and I am hurt. I fail and I stumble. And yet, I am strong. I am resilient. I am capable. Imperfection has made me human, has made me real, and has prepared me for the life I am building.

So yes, I'll continue to chase my dreams, love fiercely, work hard, and give generously but I'll also continue to embrace my imperfections. I will no longer let the pursuit of perfection define my self-worth. I will make mistakes. I will learn. I will grow. And I will do all of it imperfectly... because that is the only way to live fully, to love deeply, and to create a legacy my children can inherit with pride.

Imperfection is not weakness. It is power. It is freedom. Hell, its fucking life.

Chapter Thirteen

Re. Soul

Deeply Rooted

It's been tough. Some days, the weight of all these emotions feels like it could crush me. Every time this man leaves, I'm left in tears, aching, hoping for a change that never seems to come. We keep going in circles arguments over trivial things, miscommunications, moments of silence that speak louder than words. And I keep asking myself, if he truly cared, wouldn't he put in the effort to make things better? My heart is still heavy with love for him, even as he rejects me in subtle and not-so-subtle ways, seemingly content with the status quo.

I remind myself that he's grappling with his own struggles, but that thought brings its own conflict. Am I being selfish for wanting him to show up for me? For us? The mental tug-of-war is exhausting. Part of me wants to fight for us, to believe that we can overcome this. But the other part knows the hard truth: I can't do it alone. I can't carry the weight of fixing someone else's brokenness while trying to protect my own heart. And yet, the longing for connection, for love, keeps growing stronger inside me.

Then came a moment of temptation. An old friend reached out, offering a glimpse of the freedom and joy I've been craving. It was just a message, but it felt like a door opening to something lighter than the heaviness I live with every day. I responded, if only to taste a breath of that freedom. It was a slippery slope, and in that moment, I didn't stop to consider the consequences. I just wanted to feel alive outside of the storm of my marriage.

Reality, as it often does, came crashing back. Mr. called, asking about the kids. The moment I heard the excitement in their voices, their laughter and chatter as they prepared for the day with him, guilt washed over me. He might not be perfect, and he may not meet my needs the way I want, but he clearly loves them. That small gesture—taking time away from his work to be present in their lives—reminded me that he does have a heart, even if he struggles to show up for me.

I watched them grow attached to him and realized something important: they deserve to have that connection, even if it complicates my emotions. Despite the flaws, despite the pain, I was willing to forgive and give him a chance not for me, but for them. Protecting my children sometimes means putting my own feelings aside, even when it hurts.

Later, as I prepared for my date an old friend, a sense of hope flickered inside me. Maybe

Deeply Rooted

there's still a chance thing could change with Mr., maybe the man I married could find his way back to the love I know he has somewhere inside. I texted my old friend, but my heart was heavy. Did I really want to risk everything for a night of distraction? Could I even allow myself to escape for a moment when the truth of my marriage still lingers so strongly in my chest?

In the end, I stayed true to myself. I reached out one last time to my friend to let him know I wouldn't make it. The choice felt right, even though it wasn't easy. Focusing on the path, my children, my heart felt like the only thing I could truly control. In the quiet of my room, makeup still smudged from earlier tears, I paused. I breathed. I allowed myself a moment of stillness, reflection, and acceptance.

It's not over and maybe it never truly will be. But in that moment, I made peace with my choices. I chose patience over impulse, clarity over distraction, and my family over temporary relief. I chose to honor my heart, even while it felt lonely and uncertain. And in that quiet, I realized something important: resolution doesn't always mean closure. Sometimes, resolution is simply standing firm in your truth, no matter how complicated life becomes.

Deeply Rooted

This was a struggle for me because a part of me knew I wasn't happy, but I wanted to be. A part of me wanted to keep ignoring all the signs of betrayal and still get my fairytale ending. I wanted so badly for things to work that I convinced myself they already were. But on the other hand, I couldn't deny the truth: I was still a broken soul. A soul longing for something I had never experienced. Real safety. Real love. Real consistency.

In many ways, I was forcing myself to feel happy in my marriage. Pretending I wasn't emotionally harmed. Desperate to feel something different. I thought remaining solid staying loyal, staying patient, staying committed would eventually reward me with peace. But instead, it kept me stuck in survival mode.

Growing up, I experienced so much pain and emptiness, and I never wanted my children to feel that same void. I watched my mother constantly be disrespected, beat on and diminished, and I could never understand why she stayed. Maybe she was deeply scarred from her past. My family is secretive when it comes to certain things, so I may never fully understand her trauma or her choices.

Deeply Rooted

For many years, I blamed my mother for a lot of what I experienced. But now, with time and reflection, I see it differently. Maybe she did the best she could with what she had. Maybe we shared the same dream and just wanting to feel wanted so badly that we accepted the unacceptable. Ignoring how it might affect our children.

That fear of loneliness... that desperation for love... it's a dangerous addiction to carry.

Although my mother was on drugs most of the time, I can't help but remember that she was human too. She had her own story—whether she ever chooses to tell it or not. And maybe, in her own broken way, she was surviving the only way she knew how.

I know I deserve better. I know I deserve something safe, something steady. But the truth is, I became accustomed to the bullshit. Chaos felt familiar. Pain felt predictable. So, I chose to stick it out with Mr. because I told myself we were all fucked up just trying to survive and give our babies something we never had.

Mr. isn't my children's biological father, but he's been a father figure for most of their lives. They love him, no matter what. And in a way, I felt selfish even considering taking that away from them. I thought staying meant stability. I also thought endurance meant strength.

But now... shit feels different.

He's hurt me too deeply. The love isn't as strong anymore. I'm changing and I'm growing into a new soul, a new version of myself, one that sees clearly, feels deeply, and refuses to keep bleeding just to keep others comfortable.

Still, I can't ignore the truth: I am who I am because of my past. That brokenness still lives in me. That instinct to accept stupid shit just to feel temporary relief still whispers sometimes. Even when I know better.

This chapter *Re. Soul* isn't about pretending I'm healed. It's about acknowledging that I'm still human and I'm still healing.

I am learning to live and love life even though I'm still deeply broken at the root. I'm also learning to be patient with myself.

Right now, I'm accepting Mr. having access to me for the sake of our family but I no longer feel obligated to place our relationship above my happiness. That shift alone has changed everything. I'm not moving out of fear anymore. I'm moving with awareness.

Just because I chose not to go out with my old friend doesn't mean I'm choosing my marriage over myself and to be real I just don't have the energy for the unnecessary drama while I'm still learning how to stand on solid ground. at least for now

But inside... I'm a whole new person.

I'm moving differently. Thinking differently. I'm no longer chasing validation, begging for consistency, or proving my worth through loyalty that costs me my sanity. I don't need revenge to feel whole. I don't need to hurt anyone back to heal myself.

I'm learning that boundaries don't have to be loud to be firm.
They don't have to come with ultimatums or destruction.
Sometimes boundaries are quiet decisions internal shifts that change how much access someone has to your heart.

I can set emotional boundaries and still keep my immediate family intact.

Deeply Rooted

Re. Soul

I didn't fold.
I stayed too fucking long
in places that were breaking me.

I called it love.
Called it loyalty.
Called it "holding shit down."
But really
I was just scared to be alone
with my own thoughts.

I let shit slide.
Charged shit to the game.
Then motherfuckers tried to destroy me
and still placed the blame
on me… Fuck outta here

Deeply Rooted

Daddy touching parts of me
he never should have had access to

Destroying my body,
my spirit,
and my peace.

Will I ever be okay?

That's the question
I ask myself daily.

I was taught to survive, not to feel.
So I swallowed pain like it was normal.
Smiled through trauma.
Showed up bleeding
and called it strength.

My soul been tired.
Tired of begging to be chosen.
Tired of proving my worth to people

Deeply Rooted

who only saw me
when they needed something.

Tired of loving motherfuckers
who only loved me halfway.

I been rooted in trauma,
raised in chaos,
watered by abandonment
and somehow they still expected me
to bloom beautifully

They fucked with my trust.
They fucked with my head.
They fucked with my heart.

And every time I tried to leave,
I talked myself into staying
because,
"What if this time is different?"

It wasn't.

Deeply Rooted

I lost myself trying to be everything
the good woman,
the ride-or-die,

the strong one.

But Nobody ever asks the strong one
if she's okay.

So now?
I'm choosing me.
Not loudly.
Not dramatically.
Just intentionally.

I don't need revenge.
I don't need closure.
I need distance.
I need boundaries.
I need my soul back.

This ain't healing yet
this is the ugly growing stage

Deeply Rooted

The part where you still miss them
but love yourself enough
not to go back.

I'm not soft right now.
I'm not open.
I'm learning how to sit in my shit
without letting it swallow me whole.

I'm re-souling.
Re-building.
Re-claiming every piece of me
I gave away
just to feel loved.

so if that makes me cold hearted
so fucking be it.

Deeply Rooted

Chapter Fourteen

Meme's Prayer

Deeply Rooted

Father God, I come to You today with everything.

I know throughout life most of us come to You whenever there's a problem or sometimes just to give thanks but today, I want to lay it all out.

Many times, I feel unprotected, and I've even doubted my faith. However, I know you're real, and I know you've got me no matter what. I understand that we're not supposed to question Your plans, but I really don't understand them right now.

I wasn't raised in a church home. We used to go to church every blue moon or on Easter Sundays. I never really understood the Word or even how to pray. But the older I got; I started going based on how I felt.

But Now I don't know how I'm supposed to feel or if I'm doing this right.

I understand we all go through things, and I get that many of us share similar stories, but how is it that everything I pray for, I'm given the opposite?

Please help me understand your plan for me

Deeply Rooted

Don't get me wrong—I am beyond grateful for everything I've been able to accomplish. But what about the things I feel I really need, like love? I love my kids, and I know they love me, but what about companionship? What about love from my parents? Am I not allowed to want that? Why do I feel so alone? Why does everyone keep turning their backs on me?

I don't get it. I find myself alone every time I'm facing something really difficult—something I'm not even sure I'll survive. Why am I always in so much pain? Why can't I get anything right?

Sometimes I feel like I'm always chasing love for all the wrong reasons. Maybe it's because I don't know what real love feels like. Not even self-love. I can't feel anything but pain, and I don't understand why. I can't catch a break.

I wake up every day and I pray. I pray throughout the day and at night. I pray when I'm happy and when I'm sad. But I still can't seem to get it. Why am I still in so much pain?

I'm tired of the pain.
I'm tired of being disappointed.
I'm tired of feeling betrayal.
I'm tired of seeking revenge on anyone who's

Deeply Rooted

hurt me.
I'm tired of being strong for myself and my kids.
When will it all let up?

I'm tired of having daily meltdowns but still pushing through. I'm tired of struggling and fighting just to survive every day.

God, I'm begging for forgiveness. Whatever I've done to deserve this, I'm asking You to forgive me. I don't know if I'm strong enough to survive another heartbreak. It's too painful, and the weight is heavy on my heart.

Father God, I'm asking You to cover me. Cover my children. I'm begging You to release these demons that are attached to me. Forgive me if I'm not using the proper words, but You know what I'm trying to say.

Lord, I need You every day, so please don't give up on me. I know I'm a lot to handle, but I promise I'm working to become better. I need Your guidance. I need to feel Your love.

I ask for signs, and I guess I'm getting them—but it hurts that the outcomes are always unsatisfying. I don't know what else to do. I've given everything I had to give to my marriage, and he still seeks comfort in other women. I

Deeply Rooted

read that I'm not supposed to give up on my marriage, and I tried to honor my vows—but I don't know what else I can do. He's breaking me, and I can't bear the pain anymore.

I'm trying to stay out of trouble, but it feels like I can't get myself out of situations that pull me back into the hustle—the things I know how to do just to survive financially. I'm begging You for some kind of relief.

I know I cry rivers to You, and sometimes it feels like You're not listening. But deep down, I know you hear me. I do trust Your timing, so I'll continue to be patient—but Father God, I'm going to need a lot of strength to get through this.

Thank You for listening to me vent.
I love You.
And I thank You.

In Jesus' name I pray,
Amen.

Trusting God When You Feel Lost

Proverbs 3:5–6
"Trust in the Lord with all your heart and lean not on your own understanding; in all your ways submit to Him, and He will make your paths straight."

Chapter Fifteen
Me vs. Them

Deeply Rooted

Deeply Rooted

I don't know why I keep having this feeling that it's me against the world. I know that may sound weird, but that's just how I feel. If it's not something with my own relatives, it's my husband's family.

I remember when me and Mr. first started hanging out and his grandmother wanted to meet me. At first, I was a little shy and didn't feel comfortable, but he told me that she was cool and that I had nothing to worry about. We drove about an hour and a half to their home. She cooked for us, and we sat and had dinner. She was really sweet, but I could sense that his grandfather didn't care for me too much. Overall, it was a good visit.

A few months later, I was going through an eviction, and he reached out to his grandmother to see if she had any property available for rent. Although I knew he meant well, I didn't ask him to invite his family into my problems, so I was feeling a type of way. He called me up and told me that his grandmother was willing to help and that she wanted to speak with me first.

I pulled up to his mother's apartment, which was right across from his. As I walked in, his grandmother was waiting for me in one of the bedrooms so we could talk in private. It was me, him, his mom, and grandmother talking until both his mom and grandmother directed him out of the room. I found it strange and hella uncomfortable, but I didn't want to make a big deal out of it.

At the time, I figured they just wanted to help me, and I didn't want to be homeless with my kids, so I was open to the assistance. I guess their intention was to have some kind of "woman-to-woman" conversation and maybe they were genuinely concerned but that wasn't even close to being the case.

As I sat at the foot of the bed, his grandmother picked up a bowl of cotton balls and began to ask me questions regarding my past marriage, my kids' father, how I was making money, my credit, and more. I wasn't sure if this was part of a plan, but as I answered each question, she would give me this blank stare, then cut me off and tell me about an exercise she did whenever she felt someone was lying to her. I didn't understand it at first, so I laughed it off. She continued to question me, and every time I answered, she would throw cotton balls at me.

I didn't want to disrespect his grandmother or his mom, so I just sat there and allowed them to scrutinize and judge me. Eventually, she

Deeply Rooted

stopped, but as soon as I left that room, I told my dude what had happened and also told him that I would appreciate it if he didn't speak on my situations to his family again. After that, I never really spoke to anyone in his family and continued to do what I needed to survive.

Me and him were still doing our thing, but I couldn't remain stable in a place. One day, we agreed to move in together, but his mom and grandmother put a stop to that and ended up helping him get into a place with his ex-girlfriend who they were fond of at the time.

I remember driving around the city in my jag that was in repo at the time, looking for places to stay. I had no money, no friends, and no family to call. I would drive from hotel to hotel parking lots so my kids could sleep. During the daytime, I would use the casino daycare to place them while I hustled up a few dollars for an actual room. I didn't call anyone because I was too ashamed, and I figured all they would do was gossip instead of helping anyway. My aunt would always come through, but I felt like she was tired of helping my ass, so I didn't reach out at that time.

I called my mom after a few weeks, and she told me to just send the kids to her. I agreed, and my brother and sister drove to Vegas from California to pick them up. I'll never forget that day it was the worst feeling in the world. I didn't want to be without my children, but I had nowhere for them to go, and as a mom, I felt like a failure. That emptiness was in full effect.

In the back of my mind, I kept telling myself it was just temporary. I continued to sleep in my car for a few more weeks, but I didn't have the kids, so I wasn't really tripping. I was on my grind, and the days went by fast. I would make dancewear and swimsuits during the day and drive around most of the night to local dance clubs, dropping off pieces to clients. I knew a lot of people, but I didn't volunteer any personal business. I also felt like I needed to keep up a certain image, so I pretended I had it all figured out—even though, in reality, I was fucked.

Eventually, I connected with a guy who offered me an abandoned house to stay in while I got my shit in order. He told me that he owned the house and all I had to do was remodel it and I could live there. He was the dad to one of my old friends back in Cali, so I thought it was cool, but that was far from the truth... At this time, Mr. didn't have a place either, because things didn't work out with the apt he was in.

so we cleaned it up and moved in. I was ready to get my kids back, but my mom told me that their dad came to pick them up and was now refusing to give them back. I was furious. Just out of the blue, this MF decided to take them after months of being nowhere to be found. I couldn't report it or call the police because I had a little warrant I wasn't ready to face. He held my kids from me without any contact for six months. I made several attempts to reach him, but he kept changing his number so I couldn't contact him. I was stressed every day about my kids. Couldn't function for shit.

At the time, I didn't have all my shit together, but I had a place to stay, and that was all that mattered. I knew the only reason he wanted them was because I had to send them to my mother's for a little bit, and I knew he didn't trust them being there at all because of my past experience and he knew that my mom was still battling with drugs on and off. but that wasn't even the case. This dude only wanted the kids so he could get welfare assistance and claim them on his income taxes, and of course, show off to his girl at the time. Him getting the kids was not out of genuine concern, and a part of me feels like I played a role in that shit.

Deeply Rooted

I continued to promote my brand and sell my swimsuits, but I wasn't really getting anywhere. I shared this home with my dude, his cousin at one point, his ex at another, and whatever family member needed a place to stay for a few days. It was our own little trap house. We worked on our brand day and night. At the time, we never admitted to being in a relationship, telling people we were just business partners and had separate rooms, but we would sleep together every day. I landed the spot, and he was homeless, so we just decided to thug it out together.

We had no furniture, so his grandmother gave us an old sofa and dining table. He had a bed, and I made a pallet on the floor of my room. I held the master with the shower, so we were in my room most of the time over his bed. It was weird, but anyway… We lived in that squatter house for about two years. Throughout this time, we found all kinds of ways to make money and build our brand, but we kept falling back down and part of the problem was his family.

These people only started to come around whenever we had something dope going on and they wanted feel important, we started selling Hella merchandise and hosting our own event and They only wanted to participate in the fun stuff, never the hard work. Most of the time, he was still looking to me for the next opportunity or resource. His grandparents still didn't approve, so they stayed away. They would host family gatherings for birthdays and holidays, but I was never invited and had to stay back. Even though me and him were tight and basically a couple, he was specifically instructed not to bring me but could take other lady friends. Truth is, they never liked me, and I really didn't give a fuck. I remember around one Christmas time going shopping for his entire family and them having an entire weekend planned out and I still wasn't invited but his other female friend was although I bought all the gifts, now that shit was wild so yeah when I say I didn't give a fuck I mean that...

After we got married, they tried to welcome me in a little, but not enough to make me feel truly part of the family. I started to get invited to some family events, but not all. Eventually, they began to accept me, and for a minute, I thought I was part of the family. But then there were still times when his grandfather would get skyboxes at sports events comped from his job or the family would go on a mini getaway, and everyone was invited except me. I remember blaming my husband for not speaking up or protecting us against his family, but truthfully, he didn't care, and I would continue to fight to be accepted.

One day, my husband decided to take me to one of the events, and from that point on, he never left me or my kids out. It took a while, but I thought he was finally getting it. His mom was still weird though she would only pretend to be cool just enough to get something from me or him. Even she began to realize that he" Trying" to put us first, so she would play nice to keep whatever benefits he had to offer but she never really gave a fuck about anyone other than herself. Her actions were expected. I just hated that she would come up with lies to get him to side with her against me.

I mean, this lady really mastered the art of manipulation. She would gossip to the rest of the family, so they'd have more reasons not to like me, even though she was lying about everything. I guess that's where he gets it from. Lame as hell, but whatever.

Funny thing is, they all actually started messing with me the moment they needed something. There were times when I had temporary custody of his sister's kids when she didn't want them, I helped his brother, his sister, his mom, even his grandparents. I ran errands, picked up kids, cooked meals, cleaned houses, bailed them out of bullshit and more Like I their worker or something. I did all of it. And every single time, the second lies were being spread, they folded on me. Suddenly, I was the problem. Suddenly, nothing I did mattered.

I've come to realize that no matter what I do, these people will always be ungrateful. They will never like me. And the truth is—it was never about them. It was never about gratitude. They didn't care who I was or what I sacrificed. It was about control. It was about power. I married Mr., so I expected him to stand up for me. To protect me when his family stepped over the line. To defend me when lies were being spread. But he didn't.

He let them mistreat me. He disregarded everything I'd done for them when nobody else showed up. And it hurt, because I had always believed that the ones you ride for, the ones you hold down, are the same ones who'll be there when you need them. But that wasn't the case. I did my part. I showed up when they needed me, even though the energy was never reciprocated.

Deeply Rooted

And don't even get me started on his friends. They pretended to like me, smiled in my face, but they were always looking for ways to throw me under the bus. Little comments, "advice" that was really criticism, always comparing me to someone else, always sizing me up. Every move I made was dissected. Every choice I tried to make for my kids or myself was criticized. They acted like they had my back, but it was all for their own entertainment, their own ego.

I do blame him for not speaking up for me, for letting me fight battles alone that should never have been mine. He always made it about me, about my temper, my "attitude," my inability to "see things the right way." Never about him. Never about the fact that he let his family treat me like I wasn't even human. I was always the outsider. I was always the problem.

Even when I was kind, even when I showed up, even when I sacrificed everything, they treated me like I owed them more. And I did it all anyway. Because I'm too damn loyal. Because I thought love meant giving everything, even if no one gave a shit about me in return.

But I'm done. I'm done bending to please people who will never appreciate me. I'm done

Deeply Rooted

staying silent while they spread lies. I'm done holding my tongue while my heart breaks in a hundred little ways. I am me versus them. And in this fight, I don't apologize for being strong. I don't apologize for standing my ground. I don't apologize for knowing my worth, even when the people around me refuse to see it.

I learned something hard through all this: Some people thrive on your struggle. Some people only care about what they can take from you, and they don't care who they hurt in the process. And some people you expect them to protect you, to defend you, to love you unconditionally—don't.

And I loved him. So, I loved them because they were apart of him. I gave them the benefit of the doubt over and over. I forgave. I tolerated. I tried to prove them wrong about any negativity they heard about me

I've realized now that it's never personal—it's just how they are. But me? I'm different. I won't bend for them anymore. I won't let them define my peace. I won't let them touch my spirit. I won't let their envy, their jealousy, their manipulation steal my joy. I am choosing me. Every day, in every way. I am standing in my own truth.

Deeply Rooted

And if that means being alone sometimes, so be it. If that means cutting ties, so be it. If that means walking through the fire while everyone else watches, so fucking be it. Because I've survived worse. I've survived emotional abuse. I've survived manipulation. I've survived betrayal. And I've survived loving people who refused to love me back.

I'm done sacrificing myself for people who don't see my value. I'm done waiting for validation and I'm done hoping that one day they'll change I am my own protector. I am my own family. And that's enough.

So, it'll always be me versus them.

But I'm not the same girl they tried to break, and I don't need their approval to win.
I'm already winning— **just by staying true to myself**...

Chapter Sixteen

Self-Love Over Survival

Deeply Rooted

Even after all of that, even after surviving homelessness, squatter houses, and family drama, Mr. still found ways to hurt me by using my trauma as his weapon...

I remember nights where I'd lie awake, my mind racing. Part of me wanted to confront him about the new lies I'd discovered. But the stronger part of me knew better. Confronting him never worked. It only fueled his fire. So, I stopped. I learned to choose my battles, because at that point protecting myself and my children became priority one.

But the pain didn't go away. It stayed—heavy and unrelenting. I kept thinking, how can someone you loved, fought for, and sacrificed everything for turn into a stranger right before your eyes? It hurt knowing that all my loyalty and love meant nothing to him. I had given him everything, and in return he found comfort in other women. Same story. I know. *Sigh.*

But I refused to let that define me anymore. I realized my worth wasn't tied to his recognition or affection. I had been so focused on trying to make him happy, trying to keep us afloat, that I forgot to nurture myself. I forgot that my love,

Deeply Rooted

my time, my energy, and my patience were valuable.

That's when I began reclaiming my power.

I started small. I stopped reaching for his validation. I stopped trying to win battles I wasn't going to win. I allowed myself to cry, to feel the hurt, and to grieve the version of us I had imagined. And slowly, I began to focus on me.

I poured myself into my children, into my brand, into my creativity. I reminded myself that I had survived worse and that my strength was something no one could take from me. I practiced self-love in ways I never thought I could: refusing to be disrespected, setting boundaries, and speaking my truth unapologetically.

At the same time, I realized forgiveness was necessary—not for him, but for me. Holding onto resentment would only keep me chained to the pain he caused. Letting go, even just a little, allowed me to breathe. To live. To focus on the life, I wanted to build—not the chaos he wanted to drag me through.

That was the moment I understood something real: love isn't a war. Love isn't pain. Love

Deeply Rooted

isn't compromised at the cost of yourself. Love is care, respect, and mutual growth. And if someone can't give that—even if they once did—they aren't worth the struggle.

It wasn't easy. Some days still aren't. But every day I remind myself that I survived everything else. I can survive this. I am worthy. I am enough. And I will not settle for anything less than the love and respect I deserve—for myself and for my children.

In the chaos of betrayal, heartbreak, and disappointment, I found clarity. Even if the world felt like it was against me, I still had me. I still had my truth, my courage, and my voice. I still had my ability to rise above, to create, to thrive. And that realization—my unshakable strength—was mine forever.

Chapter Seventeen
Diamond Necklace

Deeply Rooted

So again and again, I kept telling myself that I was over this relationship and that it was officially over. And every time I told myself that, I allowed him to come back. He always had some sort of hold on me. I just couldn't let him go, no matter how bad he hurt me. I always made excuses for his actions and forgave him. I never wanted our family to break, and I always wanted this fairytale ending. I mean... don't we all? But that's never the case.

I wanted him so bad that I was willing to give up any and everything. I remember even thinking, *look, fuck our fake ass families, fuck these so-called friends and lets just move away, and start a whole new happy life.* All sounds good, right? But it's never that simple for someone who never had real intentions of making you a priority or actually wanting to be in a relationship with you. I mean, this dude literally just been playing in my face the whole damn time.

I prayed about it, cried about it, argued, and so much more. The truth is it just never was intended for us to work out. Yeah, it took a whole lot for me to get it, but I think I'm finally getting it.

Deeply Rooted

Another year passed, and Christmas was arriving. I had just received a little settlement from a work injury. And per usual, anytime I have some money, shit is going well. But this time, I'm like, *okay, let's do more with the money this time. Let's start looking into some property to invest in.* We even played with the idea of investing more into our companies—mine was the boutique, his was starting a logistics company at the time.

This time around, I actually thought things were going to work out. I remember going out Christmas shopping, and him asking me what I wanted for Christmas. He was indecisive because he felt like I had everything I wanted already. So, I told him that I wanted a diamond ring, I had actually been asking for a while.

He's never really proposed to me, and the shit was already toxic AF, but for some reason, I still felt like I deserved a ring at the least. Now, he'd gotten me other rings before, but it really wasn't like a wedding ring or anything serious, and he always made that clear. It was just like, *here, shut up.* And it always made me feel some type of way. But at the same time, I was like, *fuck it, maybe this is the best that he can do.* I genuinely tried to understand his point of view, giving him grace again.

Deeply Rooted

I honestly couldn't tell you half of the things going through my brain at the time, but I do remember always thinking he's been through a lot, at least he's trying, and I guess that was enough for me.

But anyway, he kept saying, *I'm not getting you no damn ring.* And I'm over here thinking to myself, *yeah, okay… I mean, we have the money, so what's the excuse now?* Everything was going well. We were looking to buy a house together and start this new life, so like, what is the problem? I mean, we're already married. I'm just asking for a fucking ring.

But the truth is, he wasn't into me at all.

I remember going through the mall, shopping for the kids, and he went into a jewelry store and told me to walk along. I got Hella excited, thinking, *oh, okay, he's listening. He gets it.* He always gave me a hard time right before giving me what I wanted, so I thought this time was one of those times. I kept walking. We went our separate ways. I went and bought him the shoes he wanted and everything else he picked out.

I was in a happy mood because he was getting me the ring I had been asking for. We met back up, and he had a bag in his hand from the

Deeply Rooted

jewelry store. So I became even more excited. Excited. I didn't want to put too much onto it, but in the back of my mind, I was just like, *yeah, I got my ring.*

Christmas day:

We opened our gifts and were just having a good time. But I remember having really bad anxiety because I knew I wanted this ring so bad, and I knew how disappointed I would be if he didn't give it to me. Yeah, I was bratty but so what. I wanted what I felt I deserved. I was really nervous. I don't know why, but I was really, really nervous. The kids were opening their gifts; they handed me mine. I started opening it slowly. And as I opened this box… it was a necklace. A diamond necklace.

Yes, it was beautiful. But it wasn't what I wanted. I was pretty disappointed. And he immediately pointed it out, telling me how unappreciative I was. I know it probably made him feel really bad. But in the back of my mind, I'm just like, *dude, will you ever get it? Is it really that hard for you to buy me a ring? Do you really plan on us being together and working things out? Do you want this to work at all?*

I put the necklace on for the day. It was nice. But the next day, I kind of took it off because I was in my feelings. Even though this necklace was really pretty, I just wanted my ring. I felt like he didn't appreciate me, and the arguments we were having didn't make things better. I started to question: *what the fuck are we doing here? One minute, you're making it seem like we're willing to change, and we're going to do this shit the right way despite our past. The next minute, you show me that you don't give a fuck. This isn't your vision. This isn't your ending. You're just here to do the bare minimum, just satisfying me enough until you find what you actually want.*

So, I started questioning him. I asked, *hey, are we really going through with this? Is it a good idea to move forward with purchasing a home together?* Instead of sitting down and having an adult conversation with me, he would just ignore me.

Now we're arguing, and now he's running. That started to become every single weekend.

I planned this trip to Cabo for us because I wanted us to get away. I wanted us to experience something new together. It was his first time out of the country, so I wanted to give

Deeply Rooted

him that. I wanted to have a good time. I've been to Cabo before, but he's never been anywhere. I thought a new scenery was necessary to clear out some of the tension. We both love being on the water, so I planned for us to ride camels, be out on the water on a yacht stay at a nice Airbnb, see some beautiful scenery... you know, just experience some beautiful shit.

I thought he was excited about all of it, but then he showed signs that he wasn't. And the closer it came to going, he started to pull back. So, I was like, *fuck it. I guess I'm going on this trip by myself over wasting all this money.*

A week before the trip I remember him being on the phone with somebody right before picking another fight with me. Then he left the house at like 2 o'clock in the morning and didn't come back till the next day. When I got up the next morning I found him in his car in the garage sleep. He usually does shit like that when he doesn't want to face me. The next day, he went to work, and I went through his pockets. I found a box of condoms. I immediately texted him, going the fuck off. His response was for me to stay out of his business.

Deeply Rooted

At that point, I was pretty frustrated and over it all. eventually came on the trip with me, and we had a really great time Toxic shit at its best. After we came home, things were back cool, but then I felt a little more of a drift.

One day, my daughter came to me, excited, showing a picture of her in in a HEAL program she participated in at school, As I looked at it, I saw a woman he used to mess with. I then showed my husband the picture saying, look *who Chanel's teacher is.* His response was, *oh, wow,* and nothing else. I didn't think much of it.

The next day, dropping my son off at school, I noticed him Texting that same woman. I didn't want to argue so I left it at that.

When we got home, He went to the sofa and fell asleep because he had drunk too much alcohol too early on the day. So, we never got the chance to talk about what I had just saw.

The next morning, he wanted to take me and the girls to eat. His brother came along. We went to the mall to grab some things for my daughter's Sweet 16. When we got home, he was drunk again from drinking all day. This time he had left his phone was open, so I grabbed it. I saw the SAME woman's name in

Deeply Rooted

his most recent messages and call log. Found out he'd been back talking to her for some months now. My brain immediately went, *oh, okay, that explains the weird shit before Cabo. That explains him not buying the ring.* Everything made sense.

Instead of making a big issue, I waited until he got up from his nap. I cooked dinner, made his plate, and sat with him. Calmly, I then started asking him questions. Thinking it would be a good time to talk. No yelling, no crashing out or none of that. While he was eating, I simply said, *so, why did you lie to me?* He said, *what the fuck are you talking about now?* I said, *I went through your phone. I saw the messages between you the other woman.* He said *Why the fuck are you going through my shit?*

He immediately put his food down, laid back on the sofa, and went to sleep. He didn't want to continue the conversation. So, I went upstairs and slept.

The next day, I tried again. Calmly. I just wanted to know what we were doing before making more decisions about our life, goals, and plans. He ignored everything. He created a big argument. He bashed me, body-shamed me, told me I was the worst woman he'd ever been

Deeply Rooted

with. He said he talks to other women because they make him feel great, and I make him feel horrible.

I left the house for few hours to work on my new clothing boutique and when I had got home, He had arranged for some movers come to help him move his things. I treated it like another time he was on his bullshit, so I left it at that. He was a leaver so unfortunately, I was used to him getting his shit and leaving. This time I was too annoyed and busy to even care.

The next day, I woke up to my phone off. He had contacted our phone provider and disconnected my line. I managed to save my number and transfer my line over—but not the kids'. They were still on his plan. I also got a text from the landlord. He had contacted him, saying he no longer stood the residence. The landlord He feared I couldn't cover it alone. So, he gave me 30 notices to move even after I had proved to him that I was still able to cover rent alone. Theres no telling what else he had told him because I didn't get why he wanted me out of his home so bad. We didn't renew our lease because we were planning to purchase a home, so the landlord had rights to do what he did.

Deeply Rooted

I filed for divorce and asked for spousal support. At this time, I had my shop about to open, kids to care for, bills, 2 car notes and more... and he wasn't willing to help. He completely abandoned his obligations while splurging money on other women, liquor, and other bullshit.

Me asking for support apparently pissed him off and the games began. Two months of back-and-forth. One minute we were cool, the next, not. Confusion on both ends. He would still come to the house to see the kids, still come over for dinner, we were still having sex—but we weren't together, although we were still legally married. That time frame was so confusing. He was free but I wasn't allowed to be in his eyes. He was dealing with other women, and I started talking to other guys and He started telling me that he hated me and refused to help me or the kids. Things got worse, uglier, more disrespectful so I gave him more space. I started wearing this necklace again because I missed him, but I had started my grieving process. I wore it every day. It was a memory of our relationship good and bad so i wore it as a reminded what I didn't want any more but still missed if that even makes senses.

Deeply Rooted

Weeks had past and it was now almost time to move out of the home, and I really needed him. He admitted to being the reason me and my kids had to move so He promised that once it was time to leave, he'd help me, and the girls get into another place. But he didn't. The countdown was real—two weeks to get out—and because he was closer to this other woman. He was saying fuck me and my kids.

I Remember crying my eyeballs out in the shower and forgot to take off mt neckless he had got me and When I got out and dried off, the necklace was gone. It had fell down the drain. Nothing I could do. That necklace, the memory of our relationship, was gone.

And just like that, I no longer wanted to be with him ever again. I no longer wanted to make excuses. I didn't even want the spousal support I had filed for. I just wanted peace. I had finally blocked him, and His response was turning off my kids' phones while I was at work. He knows me not being able to contact then in case of an emergency would get to me, but all id did was make me hate him even more. Him not caring about their safety, was enough.

I unblocked him just to texted him, letting him know that I'm done with the court shit. I want my divorce, but I'm not coming after you for anything and that I'll figure everything out alone. I just wanted peace.

That diamond necklace? It was my sign. The tears, the prayer, the grief, the letting go—it told me: **this is over. You cannot do this anymore. It's time to let it go.**

Deeply Rooted

Deeply Rooted

WTF

What the fuck you thought this was?

I promise the lick back will be something you're going to feel.

Or maybe I should just take this time to heal—
but let's keep it real.

You ain't never been shit, frfr.

You played a crucial role of being the man I loved,
and for a moment I truly thought you were sent from above—
but you fooled me with your charming ways.

Mr. Casanova, right?
Fuck outta here.

Deeply Rooted

You prey on women you think have lost souls.
You manipulate in ways that make you the main goal.

And right after you get what you wanted, you treat them like shit—

like you're the main prize,

and if they "fumble" you,
it's something they'll never survive.

Like WTF.

What the fuck is really going on?

Who the fuck taught you the difference between right and wrong?

How the fuck you think life can't go on

without you?

Deeply Rooted

Boy, please.

I promise it's never that serious, but you play a good game though.

Had me believing at one point that love would eventually grow.

But that was just an illusion.
Or maybe I was just stuck in a delusion—

too desperate for love to react to the red flags.

So I ignored them.
Because all I wanted was *him*.

But not anymore.

I'm learning to heal. Learning to truly love myself—

Deeply Rooted

because I can't love anyone else or allow anyone else to love me properly until I do.

First, I need God.
Second, I need me.

My kids need me too. So, before I crash out and lose it over your lame-ass ways, it's best I let this be what it is

And that's absolutely nothing.

So yeah—fly your ass somewhere else.
Go try to fool somebody else.

Because **what the fuck** was I thinking?

ANYWAY...

Chapter Eighteen

Bad Days...

Deeply Rooted

I wake up every morning, say my prayers, drink my water, then I just sit and meditate for a few minutes before getting up and starting my day. Lately, I've been battling a lot, but I'm overcoming more than ever. I'm healing. I'm happy. I took a trip for my birthday, and it really helped me mentally. I'm at peace.

I cut my hair, by the way, and it feels amazing. A little bittersweet, but amazing. It feels like shedding old skin. I'm moving into our new home. The girls are getting settled in, and everything seems to be working in our favor. However, I still feel like my patience and mental health are being tested, and I'm really trying my best to remain positive, humble, and patient. And yeah… it's hard. I have two girls that I have to protect and provide for. My boutique isn't doing what I want it to, and I'm sure that's what every business owner goes through. But I'm in a position where I needed things to move faster. Loans? Denied left and right. Sales? Not coming through like I need them to.

I've been battling myself. *What the hell am I doing wrong?* One minute, I'm thrilled with my shop; the next, I'm wondering if I made the wrong investment, the wrong decision. I'm torn between staying here in Las Vegas or moving somewhere fresh, somewhere new, starting over. But I'm also deep into new contracts for my shop and our new home. I don't want to give up so easily. But maybe giving up on certain things isn't a bad idea. Moving towards a better direction that aligns with my goals, that will suit my daughters, that will help us thrive is what's best right now

So here I am, lying in bed, looking at the sunrise, asking God for protection. *Protect me from anything that's trying to harm me. Protect me from anything that's trying to block me from reaching my goals.* I do love it here… or is it that I'm just comfortable? Either way, it goes. I really don't want to leave, but I also know deep down that this place is no longer for me.

Mr and I decided to hold off on the divorce for now. We decided to start over… maybe be friends? I don't know. The whole situation is toxic. Confusing. Yes, we love each other, but there is so much damage. I'm not sure if we can overcome it. We get like this quite often. It's sad, but it's the truth. I feel like we love each other, but then again… what does love really to have to do with it?

He's been coming through, and I appreciate that. But I'm different now. I feel different. I'm growing mentally and emotionally. A part of me died when he left us last time. Abandoned us. This time around, I do want him around as a friend. Maybe a lover sometimes, when I'm lonely—but I'm okay with it just being me and my girls for now. I want him to do well. I see him struggling mentally, but I can't fix him. He has to help himself. I can support him, but I can't heal him.

I see that he's stuck in the same mindset he's always been in. That has never been my problem. I made it my problem because I loved him, because I wanted to be that voice of reasoning. But how could I hear someone else when I wasn't even healed myself? Insane, right?

Back to what I was saying—I feel different. I want more. like I cut my hair, I've cut ties. A lot of people. A lot of habits. A lot of old patterns. I'm ready for the new. I'm ready to grow thicker, longer, stronger, healthier. Yeah, we have our bad days, but overall, I am still blessed.

I'm so thankful. I feel more positive than I ever have in my life. I'm still battling mentally and financially, but I'm more confident that everything is going to work out. Just last month, I was in a really dark space. I tapped into some things that weren't for me. I was desperate and It scared the shit out of me, but it opened my eyes. It brought me closer to God and helped me understand and visualize what I actually want to do with my life.

This whole divorce, this relationship, parenting—all of it—has felt like I've dived into the ocean without knowing how to swim but somehow making it out alive. That shit feels scary, overwhelming, but also cleansing. Although I'm still struggling in most areas, I still feel rejuvenated.

So yeah, I have bad days. But every time I think about what I've overcome, every time I remember what God has blessed me with—love, protection, resilience—there's really nothing to be sad about. I tell myself: *love yourself. Be patient with yourself. Allow yourself to heal. Allow yourself to grieve. Allow yourself to hurt. Allow yourself to feel every emotion you need to feel in that moment. Let go. Release it. Remain positive.*

And just know… everything is going to be okay.

Deeply Rooted

I've also started to focus on the little victories, the small wins. Making a sale at the shop, seeing the girls happy, having a moment of peace in the morning before the chaos begins. I celebrate myself in ways I never did before. I notice my growth, my resilience, my strength. I even notice the small ways my mindset has shifted—how I react differently, how I pause instead of exploding, how I think before I act.

Even the little things, like cooking a good dinner, having quiet moments with the girls, going for walks, journaling—these are my victories. These are my steps forward. And yeah, sometimes it feels like I'm moving in inches instead of miles, but I'm moving. And that's what matters.

I've started imagining the future differently. Instead of stressing about what I don't have or what isn't working, I visualize what I *want*. I visualize a shop that's thriving. A home that's safe, peaceful, full of love. I see myself surrounded by friends, laughter, support. I see my daughters growing strong, confident, independent. And I see myself still learning, still growing, still evolving.

It hasn't been easy. It's messy, exhausting, and sometimes I cry myself to sleep. But again, I

Deeply Rooted

wake up, shower, and I sit for a few minutes in meditation. I breathe. reset. And I move forward, one step at a time.

Yes, there are bad days. But overall, I am still blessed. And I know in my heart that this is only the beginning of something bigger, better, and more aligned with who I am and who I am becoming.

Deeply Rooted

Chapter Nineteen
Deeply: A Life Deeply Rooted

Deeply Rooted

I often question my existence and my purpose here on earth... like, was I even meant to be here? What is my purpose? Sometimes it feels like I've been surviving more than living, fighting just to stay afloat since I was young. Every time I think I'm near my breakthrough, life pushes me back into reality—harsh, unrelenting, and heartbreaking. It's sickening. Truly.

For a minute, I thought separation was the answer. That maybe removing myself from toxic energy would bring peace. But now, I'm not so sure. Now I'm lonely, more depressed than before, with no one to call on. No one to vent to. I don't trust anyone with my emotional spirit, and I'm afraid to let anyone in. My past has shown me that people can't be trusted. They'll soak up your pain, watch you break, and then use it against you. And now... I'm battling more demons than I should have ever let in from the beginning.

Even though I stay prayed up, there are times when I question God. I don't blame Him—I just don't understand. For instance, I received a settlement and struggled with what to invest in. I knew a 9–5 wasn't for me, not physically, not mentally. My passion was in design. I'd always dreamed of opening a boutique for my brand,

Deeply Rooted

but I wasn't sure it was even possible. I prayed for days, for hours, asking God to guide me, to show me the right direction. I wanted clarity, a sign that this was the path I was supposed to walk.

So, I proceeded to open my boutique. And I *knew*—I just knew—that everything was going to work out. At least, I hoped it would. But life... life had other plans.

Right before I was able to complete the build-out, my hateful ass husband decided to move out of the home. All because I went through his phone and discovered that he was lying and cheating—again. I swear this man is the spin-the-block king. One thing he always does is run back to an ex, or someone he's messed with in the past. It's like clockwork.

I thought we were finally on solid ground, finally on the same page for once. But that was far from the truth. And honestly... I should have known better. I should have trusted past behaviors, my own instincts, my own intuition. But hope... hope makes you soft sometimes. And I depended on him, financially, to cover his share of the household expenses.

Deeply Rooted

Well, not only did he leave, refusing to help at all, he also reached out to the landlord—on some bullshit—and got me put out of our home. Weeks before my grand opening. I was a mess. Stressed beyond measure. Shaking, panicked, wondering how I was going to open the doors to my shop when I didn't even have a place for me and my girls to live. My bank account was draining fast. I had no clue what to do. I was literally stuck in shock for weeks.

But I kept pushing. I couldn't give up. I'd already invested too much to stop. I kept hope alive. I opened my store without a home for me and my daughters, low on funds, juggling double monthly expenses. Shit was crazy—but somehow, I made it through.

I found a home in the same area. The girls were able to stay in their schools. My shop was nearby. I figured these were good signs. I tried to see the favor in all of it.

But once I got settled, more bills started piling up. I wasn't making enough at the shop to cover expenses. I had to hire someone part-time to work the boutique while I took a 9–5 to make ends meet. I was working both jobs for months, and it still wasn't enough. Bills kept coming.

Deeply Rooted

Car notes. Rent. Utilities. Inventory. Everything.

Shit was getting real. Fast. I started facing evictions, the threat of my car being repossessed. I was drowning, and I could feel it. Mentally, emotionally, physically—I was breaking.

After months of trying to save everything, I was exhausted. My spirit was tired. Even though I was still pushing to save my brand, I felt my soul slipping away. My confidence waned. My fire dimmed. I started questioning everything. Was this really my dream? Or was it just a fleeting fantasy that I had convinced myself was real?

I began neglecting everything I had worked so hard for. The boutique. My girls. My home. Myself. I was tired of fighting. I no longer had the energy to keep going. I couldn't. And slowly, painfully, I came to a decision that broke me but also freed me: I was going to close my dream.

It wasn't because I didn't believe in it. It wasn't because I didn't love it. I loved it more than anything. But life had taught me that some battles aren't just won by passion—they're won

Deeply Rooted

by timing, by support, by strength you may or may not have in the moment. And I had given everything I had... and it still wasn't enough.

Sometimes I feel like I've been cursed at birth. Like my entire life has been drenched in pain. from childhood neglect and abuse to family betrayal, to abusive relationships. It feels like no matter how much I survive, how much I push forward, I never reach real relief. I stay hopeful, but hope feels exhausting when it never seems to pay off.

Like... what the fuck is really going on?

Am I not worthy of a better life experience? One where I feel genuinely happy. One where I feel safe. One where I don't constantly feel like I'm bracing for the next hit...

Sitting there, letting that truth settle in, I realized something else: I had survived. Even now, even with the weight of everything crashing down, I had survived. My children are growing beautify, I had a roof over our heads. I was able to accomplish a business goal, even if it wasn't fully successful.   I have a life and I have God.

Deeply Rooted

And sometimes, **SURVIVING IS ENOUGH.**

I have lived a life that has demanded I grow stronger than I ever thought possible. I have walked through storms that left me broken, battered, and questioning my very existence. I have survived the hands that were meant to protect me turning into instruments of pain. I have survived sexual abuse from my own father, a betrayal so deep that it carved scars into my spirit before I even knew the world. I have survived physical abuse from the father of my children, someone I loved someone I trusted, someone who promised protection but delivered fear. I have survived emotional abuse that has haunted me for years, eroding my confidence, my self-worth, and my trust in humanity.

I have carried all of this with me, sometimes like a chain around my neck, sometimes like a storm inside my mind, sometimes like a wound I thought would never heal. And yet... I am still here. I am still standing. I am still breathing. I am still me.

For years, I questioned whether I was meant to survive. I questioned whether I was meant to be

Deeply Rooted

loved. I questioned whether happiness was a possibility for someone like me. The world I grew up in taught me that survival meant silence, that showing weakness meant danger, that trusting anyone could only lead to more pain. And for a long time, I believed it. I let the people who hurt me define me. I let their actions, their lies, their betrayals, their abuse shape how I saw myself. But somewhere deep in me, a root never broke.

It was this root that reminded me that even when the world turned its back, even when my father violated me, even when my children's father hurt me, I had the power to grow. I had the power to survive. I had the power to rise. That root whispered to me that my life had a purpose, even if I couldn't see it yet.

I have walked through toxic love. I have loved someone who never truly loved me back. I have given my all to a marriage that was built on lies, deceit, and manipulation. I have cried in silence, begged for understanding, and prayed for change that never came. I have forgiven, given grace, and held hope in situations where hope was not returned. I have faced infidelity, abandonment, and disrespect, and I have done so with my heart wide open, even when my spirit begged me to close it.

Deeply Rooted

I have learned that love is not about what others give you—it is about what you give yourself. Love is not about being chosen—it is about choosing yourself. Love is not about surviving someone else's cruelty—it is about surviving with dignity, with grace, and with courage.

My Children are my light. They are the reason I breathe, the reason I fight, the reason I endure. Every tear I have shed, every sleepless night, every ounce of pain has been for them. I protect them fiercely because I know what it means to feel unsafe. I provide for them because I know what it means to go without. I teach them love and strength because I know what it means to be deprived of it. In their laughter, I find my hope. In their tears, I find my empathy. And in their love, I find the validation that my life matters, that my pain mattered, that my survival matters.

Healing has been a journey I never asked for but one I embrace fully. Healing is not linear. It is messy. It is painful. It is frightening. It is beautiful. Healing is waking up every day and reminding yourself that your past does not dictate your future. Healing is crying until there are no tears left, screaming until there is no voice, sitting in silence until you find your own. Healing is forgiving yourself, not for the people

Deeply Rooted

who hurt you, but for yourself. Forgiving yourself for allowing abuse, for staying in relationships that hurt you, for believing that your worth depended on someone else's ability to see it.

I have faced financial struggles, entrepreneurial setbacks, and the weight of providing a life for my children while trying to nurture my dreams. My boutique, the work of my heart, my vision for freedom and creation, was almost derailed by betrayal and hardship. But I persisted. I opened my doors, even when my home was unstable, even when funds were low, even when my heart was heavy with disappointment.

I have learned the power of surrender. Surrendering does not mean giving up. Surrendering means releasing the need to control outcomes, the need to force love where it does not exist, the need to seek validation from those who cannot give it. Surrendering means trusting that the universe, God, or whatever force guides you, will lead you to what is meant for you. Surrendering means saying, "I am enough, and what is mine will find me."

Through all the pain, I have discovered light. Through all the abuse, I have discovered resilience. Through all the betrayals, I have discovered wisdom. Through all the darkness, I have discovered hope. I have discovered that I am not defined by what has been done to me, but by how I respond, how I rise, how I choose to live.

I have learned to love myself for the first time in my life. Not the surface love that can be broken by a cruel word or an unfaithful hand, but a deep, rooted love that comes from understanding my worth, honoring my journey, and embracing every part of me—the broken and the whole. I love myself enough to walk away from relationships that no longer serve me. I love myself enough to protect my children, my dreams, and my peace. I love myself enough to cultivate a life that honors me, a life filled with hope, joy, and purpose.

I have learned that life is not about perfection. It is about survival, about growth, about learning to stand after every fall.

I have learned that I can be deeply broken and still be deeply powerful. That I can be deeply wounded and still be deeply loved. That I can be deeply human and still be deeply extraordinary.

Deeply Rooted

This book, my story, is a testament to the strength of women who survive, who endure, who rise. It is a declaration that pain is not permanent, and power is always possible. It is a reminder that no matter how deeply broken you feel, you can still grow, flourish, and bloom into the life you were meant to live.

I am deeply rooted. I am a survivor. I am a mother. I am a dreamer.

This is my first step to freedom and Peace.

and I am, finally, unapologetically ME, HER, EVERYTHING IM SUPPOSE TO BE!

Closing Treatment

For years I was afraid to tell my story afraid I was going to be judged because of my actions and what I continued to allow. My family kept secrets, so when I was finally ready to share my truth, I felt unsupported because they didn't want certain things exposed.

I was kind of the same way. I wanted to share my experiences so bad, but I was afraid to do it. I remember giving a tiny glimpse of what I went through, and my family didn't seem moved at all. In fact, their response was, "Girl, get over it. We all been through that."

I was in shock. Like damn—

that's not a cause for concern?

Why is this shit so common, but nobody talks about it?

Deeply Rooted

How are we supposed to help our youth if all we're doing is placing Band-Aids on the wound?

That shit is wild.

So yeah, I was scared and embarrassed. It was embarrassing because of the image I tried to create for myself. I wanted everyone to see the boss side of me—not the broken side.

But here's the truth:

The broken side is what made me who I am

I've never been surer of what I really want.

So don't be afraid to tell your story... It's truly the best therapy.

Deeply Rooted

Here's your sign to start...

Deeply Rooted

Dear Diary,

Deeply Rooted

Deeply Rooted

Deeply Rooted

Deeply Rooted

Deeply Rooted

Deeply Rooted

Deeply Rooted

Deeply Rooted

Deeply Rooted

About the Author

Jametria Mays is an author, Screenwriter, entrepreneur, and survivor who writes with unapologetic honesty about trauma, healing, faith, and resilience,
she gives voice to the quiet battles many women fight in silence and the strength it takes to keep going anyway. Jametria is the founder of KYSS Collections, a women's fashion brand built from the ground up as a reflection of self-worth, confidence, and reinvention. She writes and design for women who are still standing, even when life tried to take them out.

Contact Info:

Kyssmediagroup@Gmail.com

Instagram: @Lovekyss and @Jametriamays

FB: Jametria Jarae

Deeply Rooted

Made in the USA
Coppell, TX
17 February 2026

72282644R00128